GETTING SERVICE RIGHT

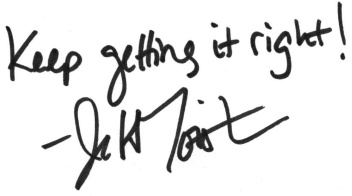

Overcoming the Hidden Obstacles to
Outstanding Customer Service

Keep getting it right!
—Jeff Toister

Jeff Toister

Keep getting it right!

[handwritten signature]

ISBN 13: 978-0-578-43336-3
ISBN 10: 0-578-43336-2

Book design: Anne C. Kerns, Anne Likes Red, Inc.

Contents

Acknowledgements

This book is a second edition, and a number of people have supported me the entire time.

First and foremost is my wife, Sally, who was the first to convince me that I really am a writer. My friend Lori Roth helped me land a book deal for the original edition and has been first in line to buy a copy of each new book I've written. My buddy Paul Herrmann has lent me countless stories from his own experiences as a customer service leader, which have made each book better. Grace Judson, my friend and editor, has worked on every book I've written and always helps me improve the clarity of my message.

Thanks to everyone who gave me their unvarnished feedback about the original book. After reading this edition, I hope you'll agree that I listened to you.

And to all my friends and family members who have supported me with your encouragement and advocacy, I appreciate all of you more than you can know. Thank you for your continued and unwavering support!

Preface

This is the second edition of *Service Failure: The Real Reasons Employees Struggle with Customer Service and What You Can Do About It*. It has a new title, updated research, and an improved focus on helping readers unravel the mysteries of getting customer service employees to be their best.

The original book was published in 2012 and went out of print in 2016. It was my first as an author, and it provided valuable and unexpected customer service lessons that I've since applied to other books I've written, including *The Service Culture Handbook* and *Customer Service Tip of the Week*.

One lesson was the title itself.

I wrote the book to help customer service leaders solve a vexing challenge: helping their employees to consistently deliver outstanding service. I imagined a title like *Service Failure* would instantly resonate with those leaders, and to a large extent, it did. The book sold reasonably well over the four years it was in print and received many positive reviews.

Yet I overlooked something pretty big—my primary customer. *Service Failure* taught me that the most important customer for a business book is an influencer who shares the book with others. It might be someone who recommends the book to a colleague or uses it to start a book club at work. Or it could be a leader who buys multiple copies and hands them out to their team so everyone can read it and work on the concepts together.

I soon heard the same feedback again and again: "It's a great read, but there's no way I'm giving someone a book called *Service Failure!*"

The title that I thought was so catchy actually hurt sales! The experience reminded me that, in customer service, we can't fall too in love with our own ideas. We have to realize that our customers may view things differently, and we need to understand them as best as we can if we want to serve them successfully.

Which brings me to another lesson.

The original book was literally a service failure. It had a binding problem that caused the pages to fall out as soon as the reader got to page 12!

I discovered the issue when I received my author's copies from the publisher about six weeks before the official publication date. I quickly alerted my editor, but by then, defective books had already been shipped to retailers. The publisher reprinted the books it still had on hand but decided not to recall the books that had already been distributed. I distinctly remember my publisher saying, "Do you know how much that would cost?!" when he defended the decision not to be more proactive.

The publisher did agree to replace damaged books at no cost if readers contacted the publisher's customer service team directly, but that required the reader to be aware of the offer. So I shared the news as best as I could via my blog, through social media, and with friends and family. My mother-in-law was one of the first people to contact the publisher in an attempt to get a defective book replaced, and she promptly got the runaround from a misinformed customer service representative.

A reader might try to return the book to Amazon or Barnes & Noble, but there was a good chance the replacement book would also be defective. I once ordered ten copies of *Service Failure* from Amazon, and five out of ten were damaged. Amazon promptly sent a replacement order, and three of the five replacements were also defective! These types of repeated problems were a sad irony that made the service failure even worse.

The situation left me feeling powerless and angry. I know many people decided it just wasn't worth their time to fix the problem. Meanwhile, it was my name, not the publisher's, on the front of the book. I'm sure that created a negative impression for some readers, even though I had no control over the book's printing or distribution.

The experience helped me empathize with what frontline customer service employees go through every day. These employees usually aren't the ones who make defective products, fail to deliver services, or intentionally decide to skimp on quality in an effort to save money. Often under-empowered and under-appreciated, these professionals face their customers' anger and try to make amends.

Getting Service Right represents a second chance to get it right. The new title is more positive, the book-binding issue has been resolved, and I've added new research and insights I discovered after completing the first edition.

It's often said we never get a second chance to make a first impression. While that's true, we can try to recover from a service failure. And we can learn from each experience, so we can make a great first impression with the next customer we serve. So whether you read the original book and had the pages fall out, or you are discovering this book for the first time, I hope this edition is helpful to you.

It's incredibly important to learn from our experiences and—as you'll see in the introduction—learning from experience is what this book is really all about.

Introduction

The man walked into a clothing store and spent a few minutes searching for khaki pants, without any luck. He finally spotted an employee and approached him to ask for assistance. "Excuse me," he said. "Do you carry Dockers?"

The sales associate, looking like a deer caught in the headlights, gazed around the immediate area and then stammered, "I don't know."

"You don't know, huh?" the customer responded. He turned and walked out of the store without waiting for a reply.

Does this sound familiar? We all experience poor customer service far too often. Many employees don't seem to care about helping their customers. Even those that do make an effort frequently miss obvious opportunities to provide better service.

It's easy to think of customer service as a matter of common sense. The sales associate clearly should have known more about the products the store was selling. And if he encountered a question he couldn't answer, he should have found another employee who could provide a knowledgeable response. Instead, he did neither. The customer walked out the door, and the store lost out on whatever money the customer had intended to spend.

This leads to an important question: why *didn't* the sales associate provide better customer service? To learn the answer, you would need the employee's version of the story.

It was the sales associate's first day on the job. He was 16 and had never worked before, so he was nervous. His supervisor had given him a brief tour of the men's department where he'd be working that day, before leaving him alone as she went on her 15-minute break. The sales associate had no training, no experience, and hadn't even met his coworkers. He felt totally unprepared and desperately hoped he wouldn't encounter any customers until his supervisor returned from her break and continued his training.

A moment later, the customer approached and asked whether the store carried Dockers.

The sales associate had no idea whether the store carried this product line. He looked around in hopes of finding the appropriate section, but had no luck. He also thought about asking someone for help, but he had no idea which of the people milling around the store actually worked there. As the customer impatiently stared at him, he unconsciously stammered, "I don't know." The response had been the customer's angry retreat.

You may have guessed by now that the 16-year-old sales associate was me. Even *I* knew what I *should* have done in that moment, but there were stronger forces at play that inhibited my performance. My lack of training made it impossible to answer the customer's question on the spot. Fear and embarrassment robbed me of the confidence I needed to act decisively to find the right answer by searching the department for Dockers or trying to find a coworker. With no experience to guide me, my instincts weren't sharp enough to prevent me from stammering, "I don't know," when that was exactly what I was thinking. The customer's impatience ensured that I didn't get a second chance.

My story is far from unique. We all know that offering outstanding customer service can mean the difference between growing your business or watching potential sales quite literally walk out your door. Yet many organizations consistently find it a challenge to get employees to serve their customers at the highest level.

There have been plenty of books written about what employees ought to do to provide exceptional service. *Getting Service Right* examines the hidden obstacles that make it difficult for employees to actually do so.

This book offers insights and guidance on overcoming these obstacles, drawing upon real stories, scientific research, and my own experiences from over 25 years as a customer service representative, trainer, manager, and consultant.

Here are just a few things you'll learn:

- How customers are to blame for nearly a third of poor service experiences.
- Why your employees might be motivated to deliver bad service.
- Why employees may not think customer service is their primary job.
- How natural instincts can cause an employee to stop listening to a customer.
- What situations can cause employees to give up on serving customers entirely.

The benefits of overcoming these challenges are enormous. Companies can develop a reputation for outstanding customer service that translates into better customer retention, increased business through referrals, and improved profitability. Service quality can easily serve as a differentiator in today's highly competitive markets.

Customer service leaders can become more effective at guiding their team's performance. In many cases, you may find that the suggestions in this book are counterintuitive or are the opposite of commonly accepted "wisdom." Knowing what really causes employees to deliver good or bad service is a key insight to apply when developing policies, writing procedures, training employees, or even making hiring decisions that will ultimately lead to better results.

Customer service employees can also gain from learning what motivates their own actions. I still recall how terrible I felt when my first customer left the store due to my poor service. Examining the reasons why I acted the way I did helped me learn how to do a better job the next time.

Getting Service Right is organized into three parts. In Part I,

"Understanding Obstacles to Outstanding Customer Service," we examine why customer service doesn't always come naturally for employees and how this can lead to poor service and, ultimately, hurt a company's bottom line. In Part II, "Overcoming Obstacles to Outstanding Customer Service," we identify and explore ten obstacles that stand in the way of outstanding service, reveal insights into why each one is an issue, and share strategies to surmount them. In Part III, "Putting Lessons into Action," we provide practical steps for implementing these lessons in your own organization.

Throughout the book, you'll find real-life examples from well-known companies, frontline employees, and my own experiences. Common service failures are dissected to understand why they happen and, more important, what can be done to prevent them. Best practices from companies famous for exceptional service are also analyzed to provide insight into how they've overcome some of these challenges.

One last word of caution as you read on. You may find yourself thinking, "There's no excuse for that behavior!" as you read some of the examples of particularly poor customer service. Of course you'd be right, but keep in mind, these stories are nonetheless true. My goal in sharing these stories is to get to the heart of why they happen. As you'll learn in Chapter 1, even inexplicably rude service may have an explanation. And once you have the explanation, you have the insight necessary to ensure it doesn't happen again. Judging by the state of customer service today, that will put you several steps ahead of the competition.

You're not alone as you explore the concepts in this book. I'm easy to get in touch with if you have a question, face a daunting challenge, or have a success story to share:

Call or text: 619-955-7946
Email: jeff@toistersolutions.com
Twitter: @toister

PART I

Understanding Obstacles to Outstanding Customer Service

CHAPTER 1

Customer Service Doesn't Come Naturally

● ● ●

Hidden Obstacles to Serving Customers

The cashier at the fast food restaurant scowled as I handed him my payment. He looked at the $5.00 bill I'd given him, glanced at the $4.05 displayed on his register, and then looked back at me asking, "Don't you have a nickel?"

"Sorry," I replied. "All I have is that $5.00 bill."

The cashier heaved a tremendous sigh, looked me in the eye, and said, "I hate people like you."

I stood in stunned silence while he counted out my change from his cash drawer and slammed the coins on the counter. "There," he said. "Now you have some cents!"

I was speechless and embarrassed. This unprovoked verbal attack was uncalled for in any setting, never mind a customer service situation. Until this moment, I never thought any employee would need to have this explained to them.

His boss was standing right behind him, yelling at employees to work faster, so it was clearly pointless to complain. However, the story soon became a favorite in my customer service training classes. Some people accused me of fabricating it since the episode was so outrageous. Others chimed in with their own stories about terrible customer service at the same restaurant.

The situation continued to bother me even as I told the story again and again. It was such an obvious example of "what not to do" that I couldn't understand the cashier's actions. What would cause a frontline employee to respond so inappropriately?

Years later, it finally hit me. Though I still didn't feel the cashier was right, I think I now understand what was behind his emotional eruption.

If you've ever been a cashier, you know what a hassle it is when you run out of change. Everything comes to a grinding halt. You wait at the register while your manager goes to the safe in the office, retrieves the change, and returns. While the manager is gone, you stand awkwardly at the register, not quite knowing what to say while the customer in front of you and the other customers in line are impatiently waiting. When the coins finally arrive, you have to break them free of their plastic wrappers and pour them into your cash drawer before you can finally give your customer their change.

Now imagine you run out of change during the lunchtime rush at this fast food place. The restaurant is crowded with customers. All the registers are open, and there's a line at least five deep at each one. The drive-through line snakes around the corner of the building, and the parking lot is full. The supervisor is clearly stressed out and frantically rushes around the kitchen, barking orders at employees, and putting everyone on edge.

This particular supervisor is likely to get even more upset if they have to stop what they're doing to get change from the office. Meanwhile, there are five impatient, hungry customers in the cashier's line who are already aggravated by the wait. Waiting a few minutes more while an angry boss fetches change from the safe is only going to make matters worse.

If you take all this into account, you can imagine that counting out 95 cents might have put this particular cashier one step closer to a bad situation he very much wanted to avoid.

I could also tell this cashier didn't like his job. I've trained thousands of frontline customer service employees over the years and often encounter people like him who are angry and frustrated. They tell me how they get paid next to nothing to deal with poor treatment from customers, coworkers, and their boss. And since they perceive that customers are the cause of most of their problems at work, many of them say their customers are the most difficult people to deal with.

This understanding made me wonder about other situations where customer service is inexplicably poor. We've all encountered employees who are unfriendly, downright rude, or ignore us completely. Some are poor listeners and don't seem to understand what we need, no matter how we explain it. Others are unresponsive and fail to return phone calls and emails or even follow through on something they promised to do. Many seem like they couldn't care less about taking care of our needs. And it's not just an isolated incident—it seems like we encounter these experiences every day!

A mentor once told me that most people inherently want to do a good job. He explained that when someone isn't doing their job well, it can take some investigation to find the root cause of their poor performance. So I started to search for hidden obstacles that prevented people from providing outstanding service.

My research revealed one very surprising truth: humans are not naturally good at customer service!

We have the potential to deliver amazing service, and some of us are better at it than others, but every person has significant obstacles to overcome. Difficult bosses, processes and procedures that don't work, and difficult customers can all get in the way. Even our own attitudes and emotions can sometimes make it hard to be great at customer service.

The biggest obstacle of all may be overconfidence. Many companies, leaders, and employees simply underestimate what's required to deliver outstanding customer service.

In this chapter, we'll look at two of the factors that hold organizations back: the challenge of consistency and a disconnect between the way companies and customers rate service quality.

The Service Consistency Challenge

Throughout my more than 25 years in customer service, I've repeatedly heard people refer to customer service as a matter of common sense. This belief belies the fact that good customer service can be maddeningly difficult to achieve with any consistency.

Companies within the same industry often provide very different levels of service. Southwest Airlines and United Airlines represent opposite ends of the customer service spectrum. According to the 2018 American Customer Satisfaction Index (ACSI), Southwest earned an 80 point customer satisfaction rating, the highest among the major airlines in the United States. United, on the other hand, was the third worst, with a 67 point rating.[1]

On the surface, it seems easy to understand why these two airlines are so different. Southwest is known for their fun-loving employees and has had books written about its exceptional service. United's customer service claim to fame is the infamous 2017 incident where a passenger named David Dao was physically dragged off a plane by airport security to make room for a United crew member who needed to get to Louisville.[2] The dragging incident, which made national headlines, was just one of a long list of viral customer service failures for the airline.

The problem with industry ratings is that they're averages, not absolutes. You're not guaranteed a great experience the next time you fly Southwest, and it's unlikely you'll be physically dragged off the plane the next time you fly United. Many disgruntled passengers have taken to calling Southwest "Southworst," and United has a loyal following of dedicated passengers who can't imagine flying with any other carrier. In other words, an average rating doesn't necessarily equate to *your* rating.

Stores within the same company may also be miles apart in their dedication to customers and offer very different levels of service. The Yelp ratings for the five Starbucks locations closest to my home range from two-and-a-half to four stars (out of five). The location with four stars has limited seating and a tiny parking lot that's often blocked by cars in the drive-through line, but the store's consistently friendly employees some-how overcome the location's physical limitations. Meanwhile, a nearby store with a three-star rating is much larger with more seating and park-ing, but the employees don't seem quite as friendly.

Customer service can even vary widely within the same store or department. My favorite Starbucks location has a three-and-a-half-star rating on Yelp, with individual reviews ranging from one to five stars. I'd give it a solid four stars, but I'm only one of thousands of customers. Two recent one-star reviews complained of extremely slow service, while a recent five-star reviewer gushed about the fast service they received.[3]

Companies, stores, and individual employees can also change. In 2013, T-Mobile had the lowest rated customer service for wireless phone carriers on the ACSI, with a score of 68. Five years later, T-Mobile led Verizon, AT&T, and Sprint, with a score of 76.[4] Service at the bagel shop in my neighbor-hood improved dramatically a few years ago when a new store manager was brought in. A server at a local restaurant I go to was very unfriendly the first time he waited on my table, but now is very friendly and even comes over to my table to say "Hi" when I'm seated in another section.

It's tempting to look at customer service as a matter of common sense, but "common sense" really means "the way I personally see it." There is no one right way to serve every customer. Companies, stores, and individual employees aren't always good or always bad when it comes to service.

Customer service is ultimately based on human-to-human relation-ships, and human beings are infinitely variable.

The service consistency challenge has to be met head-on if you want to deliver outstanding service. Companies must develop service strategies that meet the needs of a wide range of customers and invest in the right tools and training for their employees. Customer service leaders need to encourage good performance while accepting that employees can learn from occasional mistakes. Employees must develop the flexibility to adapt their approach to each person they serve.

The Customer Service Disconnect

In September 2016, the Wells Fargo website touted the company's customer-centric culture. There was even a quote from then-CEO John Stumpf that touted the organization's commitment to customers:

"Everything we do is built on trust. It doesn't happen with one transaction, in one day on the job or in one quarter. It's earned relationship by relationship."

That statement couldn't have been farther from the truth. That same month, the Consumer Financial Protection Bureau announced it was assessing Wells Fargo $185 million in fines for opening more than two million phony bank accounts and credit cards in the names of unsuspecting customers. The phony accounts were opened by thousands of employees who were pushed by their managers to meet unrealistic sales targets, and more than 5,300 employees were ultimately fired.[5]

Stumpf continued to promote the idea that Wells Fargo was customer-focused even when he announced the staggering news to the company. In his statement to employees, he said, "Our entire culture is centered on doing what is right for our customers."[6] Here was a large company facing massive fines for consumer fraud, and the CEO could not bring himself to admit that the way it treated customers was a product of the win-at-all-costs culture his aggressive strategies helped create.

The Wells Fargo example may seem extreme, but it's not uncommon. A 2017 study from the consulting firm Capgemini Group found that 56 percent of companies experienced a disconnect, wherein executives felt their company was customer-centric, but customers did not agree.[7]

For instance, the shipping company DHL ran an advertising campaign throughout 2008 highlighting its commitment to customer service. Television commercials featured various ways that DHL went above and beyond for its customers. Each closed with an emphatic tagline: "We're putting service back in the shipping business."

DHL's advertising department apparently forgot to check with the rest of the company, because its customers didn't agree. Customer service ratings continued to trail FedEx and UPS, DHL's closest competitors, and in November 2008, DHL announced it was pulling out of the domestic express delivery business in the United States.[8]

It can be difficult for executives to acknowledge a service issue in the business they manage. Gemma Leigh Roberts, a chartered psychologist, performance coach, and founder of the Career Compass Club, suggests the customer service disconnect is something many leaders unconsciously do to protect their egos.

"As an executive, you're dealing with the pressure of ensuring the business is performing effectively, and that can be directly related to how you view yourself. Challenging your perception of business performance (which you are responsible for leading) can lead to you challenging your own performance, which can be painful for your ego and damaging for your confidence. In this scenario, sometimes executives choose not to acknowledge facts or consider them irrelevant, which is a self-protection strategy. It's often not a conscious process, rather something our brains work on in the background, without our conscious knowledge."

Some executives are interested in using customer feedback to gain a better understanding of their customers. These leaders must still be careful to ensure that the way customer feedback is gathered and presented doesn't create blind spots. The data can sometimes convince executives their company is doing well while masking signs of customer dissatisfaction.

Customer service surveys are an example of potentially misleading data. As discussed earlier in this chapter, survey scores represent the average of many experiences. These averages can hide pockets of upset customers if there are enough happy customers to bring up the overall score.

The Gallup Organization published a study in 2006 that examined a telecommunications company with an 88 percent customer satisfaction rating. As with the other examples described here, this rating was the average for the company's entire call center. Things got interesting when Gallup looked at the scores of individual employees. It discovered that customers who dealt with the worst 10 percent of the reps had a negative experience nearly 60 percent of the time. These reps were creating more problems than they solved![9]

An executive managing this call center may be tempted to view the 88 percent satisfaction rating as a sign of success. However, relying solely on the aggregate survey results masks a potentially large problem. The average rating means nothing to the unhappy customers on the phone with one of the bottom 10 percent reps.

Survey scores are also subject to manipulation. Many customer service surveys contain intentionally misleading questions designed to elicit higher scores. Employees in many industries routinely engage in survey begging, a practice where employees directly ask customers for a high survey score in return for some benefit to the customer.

Customer complaints are another source of feedback that's easily misunderstood. It's estimated that only 5 percent of upset customers share their feedback directly with a company manager or executive. This makes it tempting for a manager who hasn't received any complaints to assume that customers are generally satisfied.[10]

Managers who do receive complaints don't always recognize them as a sign of a larger problem. It's tempting to write off a complaint as a one-time occurrence, even though many other customers might feel the same way. Some managers even get defensive, attributing criticism to unreasonable customers rather than poor service.

Roberts suggests subtle cognitive biases can cause leaders to quickly dismiss customer complaints and negative feedback.

"Our brains process huge amounts of data a second, and in order to do this without being overwhelmed, we need to be able to sort data and information to make decisions quickly. Our brains have the amazing capacity to do this through creating effective shortcuts, but sometimes this process lets us down, and we have to challenge our view of the situation. If an executive is used to thinking of a customer situation in a positive light, they may keep searching for evidence to support this rather than challenge their assumptions and see the new factual evidence in front of them."

Individual customer service representatives tend to overrate their abilities just as often as executives do. In a series of experiments, David Dunning and Justin Kruger discovered that the less someone knows about a topic, the more they tend to overrate their knowledge. Dunning and Kruger discovered that only people in the top quartile in terms of knowledge typically avoid overrating themselves.[11]

I've run a similar experiment many times with consistent results. I ask a room full of customer service reps to rate the customer service they personally deliver on a scale of 1–5, with 5 being best. Next, I ask the reps to look around the room and assign a rating to the entire team. On average, the reps rate themselves a 4 while rating the team a 3. The math doesn't add up—and it shows that most reps believe they're better than their peers.

Some customer service employees have a difficult time seeing where their own actions fall short, even when it's obvious to everyone else. The night before I was scheduled to deliver customer service training to employees of an airport parking operation, I did a secret shopping test at several of their parking lots. My goal was to see how well the cashiers followed the company's basic service procedures, such as greeting customers, smiling, making eye contact, explaining the parking charge, and thanking customers. The results weren't promising: four out of five cashiers failed to adhere to any of the service standards.

The next day, I started the class by introducing myself and explaining that I had conducted a secret shopping test the night before. The cashiers

I had shopped were all in the class, but none of them remembered my driving through their lane to pay for my parking. Everyone seemed surprised and even angry that four cashiers had done so poorly.

I didn't share the names of the individual cashiers I had shopped, because I didn't want to publicly embarrass anyone. However, many of the participants pressed me to reveal their identities. Some of the most vocal participants clamoring for the cashiers' identities to be revealed were the four cashiers themselves! They were so confident in their own abilities that it never occurred to them that they might have been one of the employees who did poorly. One of the four cashiers actually stood up and demanded accountability: "Who was it?! Who made us look bad?"

This disconnect reveals how hard it can be for company leaders and frontline employees to realize they have room for improvement. Corporate management, removed from their customers by layers of personnel and automated systems, will fail to take action as long as they believe everything is okay. Meanwhile, frontline employees may blame service shortcomings on dumb decisions by management, unreasonable customers, or both, while failing altogether to see where their own efforts do not measure up.

You have to be willing to get real if you want to deliver great customer service.

Natural Obstacles to Service Greatness

As mentioned at the start of this chapter, inertia may be the biggest reason why companies don't provide better customer service. If you don't think there's a problem, why should you do anything about it? However, employees in organizations that truly want to improve service levels still face significant challenges.

Sometimes the solutions to these challenges are right in front of us.

Think back to the cashier at the fast food restaurant. The cashier's fear of his manager's intimidating style, his dislike for the job itself, and his general disdain for his customers overrode any understanding of what was and was not appropriate to say to a customer who had the temerity to require 95 cents in change. As you'll learn in Chapter 10, emotions tend to overpower logic.

These factors don't excuse the cashier's behavior, which was completely out of line, but they do provide insight into how you can make sure that *your* employees will never say, "I hate people like you!" to any of your customers.

This book examines natural barriers to outstanding service and provides suggestions for navigating over, around, or through them. You'll read some cautionary tales illustrating how our natural instincts can often push us to do the wrong thing. And you'll learn about companies, departments, and individuals that have overcome these challenges to delivering consistently amazing results.

CHAPTER 1 NOTES

1   The American Customer Satisfaction Index, 2018 Airline Industry results. www.theacsi.org.

2   Victor Danile and Matt Stevens. "United Airlines Passenger Is Dragged From an Overbooked Flight." *The New York Times*, www.nytimes.com. April 10, 2017.

3   These were the ratings on www.yelp.com for the five Starbucks stores closest to my home as of August 22, 2018. As with many customer service ratings, the ratings may go up or down over time as more customer reviews are added.

4   The American Customer Satisfaction Index, 2018 Wireless Telephone Service results. www.theacsi.org.

5   Matt Egan. "5,300 Wells Fargo employees fired over 2 million phony accounts." *CNN Money.* September 9, 2016.

6   John Stumpf. "Perspective on Sept. 8 settlement announcement." Wells Fargo website, https://stories.wf.com/perspective-todays-settlement-announcement/?cid=adv_prsrls_1609_102495. Accessed September 15, 2016.

7   "The Disconnected Customer: What digital customer experience leaders teach us about reconnecting with customers." Capgemini Group. 2017.

8   Jack Ewing. "DHL to Halt Express Deliveries in U.S." *Bloomberg Businessweek*. www.businessweek.com. November 10, 2008.

9   John H. Fleming, Curt Coffman, and James K. Harter. "Manage Your Human Sigma." *Harvard Business Review*, pgs 107–114. July–August 2005.

10   John Goodman. "Manage Complaints to Enhance Loyalty." *Quality Progress*, pgs 28–34. February 2006.

11   David Dunning and Justin Kruger. "Unskilled and Unaware of It: How Difficulties in Recognizing One's Own Incompetence Lead to Inflated Self-Assessments." *Journal of Personality and Social Psychology*, Vol. 77, No. 6, pgs 1121–1134. 1999.

PART II

Overcoming Obstacles to Outstanding Customer Service

CHAPTER 2

The Customer is NOT Always Right

● ● ●

Equipping Employees to Handle
Challenging Customers

One of the most challenging obstacles to effective customer service is the customers themselves. Customer service horror stories frequently begin with the implicit assumption that the customer was a reasonable, rational, and pleasant person who should have been easy to serve. This is sometimes the case, but the reality is that there are many instances where customers play an active role in creating their disappointing experiences. As the old saying goes, it takes two to tango.

I once sat on a hotel shuttle bus waiting for my ride to the airport, while two angry women fumed because the hotel couldn't find their reservation. The bus ran on a route between the airport and two hotels a short distance apart that were run by the same company. The trouble started when the women weren't sure which hotel they were going to, and the shuttle driver radioed a coworker for help finding their reservation.

The shuttle sat in the driveway of one of the hotels, while a guest service associate explained to them that she was doing her best to locate their reservation. The hotel associate was gracious, apologized for the delay, and headed back inside to keep searching. The two women got even more agitated after the associate left, grousing about how stupid she was and swearing they would never stay at this hotel again. The shuttle driver re-boarded the bus and attempted to make a little small talk, but the women were so unpleasant that he quickly exited.

The guest service associate came back to the bus a few minutes later. "I apologize for the delay, but we finally figured it out," she said. "We checked with our other hotels in the area after we couldn't find your reservation here. We discovered it had been made at our sister hotel on the other side of town."

The two women sat in stunned silence. All this hubbub was their fault. The guest service associate gave them the option of staying at the hotel where they currently were, though she cautioned them the rate would be significantly higher. The other option was for the hotel to provide them with a complimentary shuttle ride to the hotel where they had their reservation.

But the women still weren't happy. They wanted to know why the rates were so much higher at this hotel. The associate calmly explained that rates were a function of a number of factors, including current occupancy levels, the hotel's amenities, and its location. This was a full-service hotel with a beautiful view of the bay; the other property was a limited-service hotel in an industrial part of town.

The women also wanted to know how far they were from the other property and were upset to learn it would be a 20-minute bus ride to get there. However, they ultimately decided to accept the shuttle ride and stay at the other hotel.

I was glad to finally be heading to the airport, but the whole situation left me mystified. The problem occurred because the two women made a mistake. The problem got worse because they expected the hotel to offer them a substantial discount despite the mistake having been their own. They never even thanked the guest service associate or shuttle driver for being patient or for offering them a free ride.

Unfortunately, customers like this are far too common. I've personally served more unreasonable people than I can count, and my guess is you probably have, too. So I decided to investigate what makes some customers so difficult and to discover some effective ways to serve them.

In this chapter, we'll re-examine the notion that the customer is always right. You'll see how customers actually do make mistakes, have unreasonable expectations, engage in self-sabotaging behavior, act dishonestly, and even abuse the people they expect to help them. All these customer behaviors can lead to disappointing service, but there are solutions that will help your employees overcome these obstacles.

The Customer is Often Wrong

The phrase "the customer is always right" has become a fixture in our customer service culture, but where did it come from?

Some historians attribute it to a quote from Chicago merchant Marshall Field: "Right or wrong, the customer is always right." Still others think it's a modification of a quote from the famous hotelier Cesar Ritz: "The customer is never wrong."[12]

These men were customer service pioneers in the late 19th and early 20th centuries. They introduced customer-friendly policies, insisted on high-quality products and services, and treated their employees much better than most employers of the time. Their versions of "the customer is always right" describe a successful business philosophy rather than a literal rule for doing business.

John Goodman, vice chair of the company Customer Care Measurement & Consulting, shared some insights with me from the upcoming second edition of his book, *Strategic Customer Service*. He estimates that 20 to 30 percent of customer dissatisfaction is a result of the customer making an error or having unrealistic expectations.[13] Unfortunately, many of these customers still believe the customer is literally always right. They assume that any problem is automatically the company's or employee's fault rather than accepting their share of the responsibility.

Customers like these can be angry, upset, and unreasonable. I often see airline passengers running late for a flight who loudly complain about the airport's poor layout, the disorganized security checkpoint, and the unhelpful airline employees, without acknowledging that their troubles were really caused by arriving at the airport only 30 minutes before their flight. Their anger and frustration causes them to take an intractable position when they lodge their complaint.

I once witnessed an intoxicated airline passenger loudly complaining to the gate agent about missing her flight. She had been drinking in the airport bar and was upset that she wasn't paged and nobody came to get her. Never mind that the bar was within sight of the gate, the gate agent had, in fact, called the passenger by name when announcing final boarding, and it's ultimately the passengers' responsibility to show up on time for their flight.

Sometimes a customer's mistake can be the difference between evaluating the same experience as outstanding or poor. I was scanning customer service ratings site Yelp several years ago and saw that a customer had given my local barbershop a one-star rating. I couldn't believe my barbershop merited such a low rating from anyone, so I read the review.

The reviewer felt the location was convenient and his haircut was good. He even commented on the pleasant shoulder massage the barbers give with a vibrating massager at the end of the cut. But the barbershop still received just one star because the reviewer felt the haircut was too expensive at $20. However, at the time, the barber shop was charging just $12 for a haircut, not $20.

Perhaps the reviewer would have given a four- or even a five-star rating if he had the correct price in mind. Instead, he wrote a review on Yelp that warned other customers to stay away.

Some customers simply disagree with a company's policies and expect special treatment. While eating breakfast in a café one day, I overheard a customer arguing with his server. He was upset about the café's prices and wanted a discount.

This café, like many restaurants, offers various combination plates, but also has an à la carte menu. The restaurant entices patrons to order more by pricing the combination plates lower than if the items were ordered à la carte. This patron was upset about being charged $6.95 for the eggs, meat, potatoes, and toast special even though he didn't want the potatoes. The server tried to explain that the meal was still a good deal because the items he wanted would cost more if ordered à la carte, but the customer insisted he should receive a discount. (This was several years ago, but even then, $6.95 was a terrific deal for all that food!)

The server called the manager over, and the argument continued. I admired the server and the manager for their patience and tactfulness with this unreasonable guest, but the guest was obstinate. Finally, after 10 minutes of wrangling back and forth, they settled on another selection that the customer felt was fairly priced. The customer scowled as he sat by himself and ate his meal, though he was mercifully silent. When he finished, he paid his bill and walked out without leaving a tip.

Customer service employees often feel stuck when fielding a complaint from a customer who is obviously wrong. Human nature may cause the employee to point out the customer's error, but that's usually an unwinnable argument. A much better solution is to modernize "the customer is always right" philosophy and operate by the rule that we should always try to help the customer *feel right*.

The best way to make customers feel right is to help them avoid being wrong. We can do that by creating generous, customer-friendly policies.

Starbucks considers a customer to be "any person who enters our spaces, including patios, cafés, and restrooms, regardless of whether they make a purchase." The policy was largely driven by an incident in Philadelphia, where a manager was accused of racial discrimination for calling the police on two men who were waiting for a friend without first making a purchase.[14] Yet this policy gives Starbucks employees everywhere the flexibility to welcome people without having to decide if someone has already paid or is lingering too long.

When a customer does make a mistake, generous policies can empower employees with more options to make a customer feel right.

The two women in the beginning of this chapter who arrived at the wrong hotel were offered a free shuttle ride even though the hotel was under no obligation to do so. This cost the hotel time and money, but it saved the two women a $20 cab ride and ensured they made it safely to the correct destination. The free shuttle ride helped alleviate their anger and kept the situation from escalating into a confrontation in front of the hotel.

Generous, customer-friendly policies have the added benefit of helping companies stand out from the competition.

Discount Tire provides an excellent example. The tire store chain will patch flat tires free of charge, even if you didn't buy the tire from them! This generous policy, combined with Discount Tire's fast and friendly service, can help people go from feeling stressed about the cost of unexpected car troubles to feeling relieved. Customers can often get their tire fixed and be back on the road in as little as 45 minutes, even if they didn't have an appointment. The repair service leaves an incredibly positive impression with existing and prospective customers alike, making them more likely to buy their next set of tires there.

Another important step is to train employees to avoid placing blame and, instead, to focus on finding a solution.

The Champaign Public Library is one of a growing number of libraries that are reducing and removing late fees. According to library assistant Ruairi McEnroe, giving staff more latitude to help customers avoid late fees has helped library staff feel more empowered.

"We have a process in our system whereby, if a customer claims they have returned a book but it still shows as being out, we can set the item as inactive, and the customer will not be charged any overdue fees on this item. More often than not, the customer comes back in to apologize with the item in hand a few days or weeks later. We don't judge, we tell customers it happens to everyone (including staff). With the sheer amount of items returned, everyone can be forgetful."

A big worry for customer service managers is what to do when a customer's mistake leads to a poor experience and that customer chooses to vent their frustrations in a public forum like Twitter or Yelp. The negative review can be harmful to business, but arguing with the customer online for anyone to see makes the business look even worse. Adopting the "help the customer feel right" philosophy can work here, too.

Nike's Twitter team provides a great example of how to tactfully avoid arguments and focus on solutions. When someone posted a fake Nike gift card giveaway online, many customers were duped into believing it was a legitimate promotion. Quite a few tweeted their annoyance with Nike when they weren't able to get a gift card, even though Nike had nothing to do with the hoax.

While it may be tempting to point out these people had fallen for an obvious scam, replies from Nike were professional and helpful. One example read, "We're aware of this link. That gift card giveaway isn't a Nike promotion and is being offered by a third-party company. We are working with our teams to have it removed."[15] This response provided clear facts without casting blame on the customer and also alerted other customers to the scam.

Occasionally, a tired or distracted customer will simply lose the ability to think clearly. Research from Scott S. Wiltermuth and Larissa Z. Tiedens reveals that people become more judgmental and less open to ideas when they're already in a bad mood.[16] This makes it awfully tough for the customer service representative who has to remember that the customer should always feel right!

Once again, the best solution is to avoid arguing with the customer and offer a solution instead. Here's an example from Rama, who worked as a front desk agent at a hotel in Las Vegas.

I was checking in an older gentleman when he asked me what time it was in Las Vegas. I told him it was 6:05 p.m. He told me that he didn't want the time in Los Angeles, but in Las Vegas. My response was that L.A. and Las Vegas are in the same time zone, and it was, indeed, 6:05 p.m.

He informed me that my watch was set to L.A. time because that's where all the hotel employees lived, and I should set it to Las Vegas time when I commute [to work]. After 10 minutes of going around and around with him about the time, I finally realized it was a no-win situation. I looked at my watch, which now said 6:15, and responded, "I am so sorry. You're right; I never adjusted my watch when I got to work today. It's actually 6:18." He accepted that, thanked me, and went up to his room. I knew that the extra three minutes I added in wouldn't make him too early or too late for anything, including his flight home.

Putting employees in the position to say "Yes" instead of "No" helps them avoid confrontations or arguments and allows them to focus on resolving the customer's complaint. The employees that are most successful at handling these situations make the customer feel like they're on the same side. They approach the problem as partners, rather than adversaries, and work with the customer to provide a successful outcome.

Customers Have Varied Expectations

Your customers evaluate the service you provide based on how well you meet their expectations. They believe they've received good service when you've met their expectations, poor service when you've fallen short of their expectations, and outstanding service when you've exceeded their expectations. The challenge employees face is that all customers have different expectations, and no two customers are exactly the same.

Let's consider a hypothetical example where three customers walk into their local grocery store to buy milk, eggs, and bread.

The first customer, Tina, walks into the store and quickly picks up the milk and eggs. She heads for the bread aisle, where she encounters Jim, a longtime store employee. Jim and Tina exchange hellos as she walks by, grabs the bread, and heads for the register. Tina's in and out in less than 10 minutes. All of her expectations have been met, so she'd rate her experience as "good."

Deepti walks into the store a few minutes later and quickly picks up the milk and eggs. She heads for the bread aisle where she, too, encounters Jim, the longtime store employee. Deepti pauses and asks Jim which brand of bread is the freshest today. He asks her a few questions and then suggests some freshly baked rolls from the store's bakery department that would be perfect for the sandwiches she plans to make for lunch. He walks her over to the store's bakery department and hands her the warm rolls, which happen to be on sale. Deepti's expectations were exceeded by Jim's friendly and helpful service, so she'd rate her experience as "outstanding."

Erin walks into the store a few minutes after Deepti. She also quickly picks up the milk and eggs and heads for the bread aisle, where she also encounters Jim. Erin is in a hurry, so she doesn't notice Jim smiling and saying "Hello" as she walks by. Unfortunately, Erin is in such a hurry that she drops the carton of eggs as she struggles to reach for a loaf of bread on the top shelf with her hands already full. Angry and embarrassed, she mutters to herself that the store doesn't know how to stock their bread so that people can easily reach it. She grabs the bread and heads towards the register, leaving the carton of broken eggs in the bread aisle. Erin leaves the store in a bad mood and without any eggs, so she'd rate her experience as "poor."

Jim, the store employee, took the same approach with each customer, but there were three different outcomes. His error was assuming that all three customers simply expected him to be friendly and offer assistance when asked. Tina may have expected nothing more than a friendly greeting, but Jim wouldn't know that for sure unless he had offered some assistance. Jim lucked out with Deepti, because she asked him a question that prompted Jim to provide more service. He could have saved Erin from a disappointing experience if he'd noticed her struggling to reach the bread and had proactively lent a hand before she dropped the eggs.

Sometimes, two customers view the same experience very differently. Whenever I'm in Portland, Oregon, I enjoy visiting a wine bar called Oregon Wines on Broadway, because they offer great service, feature local wines, and their bartenders often help me discover something new. I decided to write a review on Yelp after visiting a few times and was surprised by some of the reviews others had written. Many people like me rated the wine bar four or five stars (on a five-point scale), but about a third of the reviews were only one or two stars. When I looked closely, I discovered that the comments made by the high and low raters described similar experiences!

These ratings told me that the wine bar offered consistent service, but it wasn't right for everyone. The people who gave it low ratings had expected a more romantic setting with attentive servers. They were surprised by the boisterous atmosphere and disappointed by all the time the employees spent chatting with the people at the bar. Ironically, the very things they disliked were cited as positives by the people who gave high ratings.

How can you provide outstanding service if you can't be all things to all people, and customers have infinitely variable expectations? The answer lies in how you manage customer expectations and then adapt your service to meet their needs.

The first step is making informed trade-offs between doing a few things really, really well that your customers will value, and other less-valuable attributes where your company may not excel. For example, Trader Joe's received the second highest rating among grocery chains from the ACSI in 2017, with an impressive 85 points.[17]

Part of the company's success is because it offers a much smaller selection than a regular grocery store, with just 4,000 different items on average compared to 50,000 at the typical store. This makes it much easier for Trader Joe's employees to be knowledgeable about the products they sell, and it also helps the company avoid the frequent stock-outs that plague many chains.[18]

In their book *Uncommon Service*, authors Frances Frei and Anne Morriss provide an excellent process for deciding which trade-offs to make. Southwest Airlines was one example they profiled. The airline focuses on providing the attributes most desired by their core customers, such as low prices and friendly service, while trading off on-board amenities such as assigned seating and a first class cabin, which are not as important to Southwest's customers.[19]

The second step is helping customers maintain reasonable expectations. An easy way to do this is to tell customers up front what they should expect. One of my favorite local restaurants has an unusual menu, so servers are trained to ask customers, "Have you been here before?" If they say "No," the server will take a moment to explain the menu and point out other ways the restaurant is unique.

This approach works in other settings, too. Mechanics avoid misunderstandings when they provide a written estimate up front and clearly explain recommended services. Doctors make their patients feel more at ease when they describe a procedure before conducting an examination. Butchers provide extra confidence when they offer grilling tips after helping a customer pick out a few steaks for a backyard cookout.

One caveat when setting expectations is that customers tend to hear what they want to hear. If a customer drops off some clothes at the dry cleaner and are told their clothes will be ready in two to three days, the customer is likely to hear "two days." It's always better to say "three days" if that's the longest it will take. If the clothes are ready in three days, the customer will be satisfied. If they're ready in two days, you have an opportunity to exceed expectations by calling the customer and letting them know their clothes were done early.

The third step to effectively serving a wide variety of customers is to adapt your service to suit their needs.

I once visited a winery to taste some wine with my wife and parents. The first employee who greeted us was very energetic and outgoing and seemed to know a million jokes and funny lines. Unfortunately, he was more focused on putting on a good show than answering our questions about the wine.

This employee eventually became distracted by a large group of people who had arrived on a tour bus, and a second employee came over to assist us. She was much more reserved, but knew a lot about the wines she was pouring. She answered all our questions and even gave us a sample of a special wine that wasn't on their menu. As she rang up a couple of bottles of the wine we decided to purchase, I couldn't help noticing the first employee's picture on the "Employee of the Month" sign over the cash register. We all agreed the second employee's service was much better.

This experience reminded me of the Platinum Rule of customer service. Many of us have heard of the Golden Rule, which suggests that we treat customers the way we want to be treated. The Platinum Rule is an upgraded version that suggests we treat customers the way *they* want to be treated. This requires employees to listen carefully, ask questions, and adapt their service to each individual customer.

The Self-Sabotaging Customer

Customers are often their own worst enemy when it comes to receiving great service. They inadvertently—or sometimes deliberately—create obstacles for the employees trying to help them. A self-sabotaging customer may not realize they're causing their own frustration, especially if they believe the customer is always right, so they will sometimes get angrier and angrier the more an employee tries to help them.

Some customers struggle to explain what they need, especially when they're in a hurry or angry. Here's an example from Marjorie, a customer service rep for a telephone company.

One Sunday afternoon, a very angry man called. He started off telling me his 1-800 number wasn't working and then went off on a string of other issues he had. When I started trying to ask him questions about the 1-800 number, he went off on me and told me I was stupid and I obviously didn't know how to do my job. He wouldn't give me any of the information I needed to help him—just told me to figure it out.

I tried repeatedly to tell him that I needed some basic level of information to help him, but he apparently wanted me to be a mind reader. In the end, he said, "I don't care about my 1-800 number, I'm mad that my calling card doesn't work." The calling card was barely mentioned in his original tirade, but that was the one thing he wanted from the call...well, that and to berate a total stranger!

Occasionally, customers will inexplicably and deliberately give misinformation to customer service representatives. Here's an example from Noyan, who worked at an outdoor retailer.

I had a customer walk up to the counter and tell me he received a call from us stating the sleeping bag we special-ordered for him was in. When I asked his name, he replied, "Bill." I hurried back to our stock room to find his sleeping bag, but after frantically searching for almost five minutes, I couldn't find it. I then checked our call log to see which one of my coworkers contacted him, but his name was nowhere to be found on our list.

I finally realized that no one had ordered Bill's item. When I broke the news to him he was outraged and demanded I find him the item he wanted. "I'm so sorry," I replied, "but we only have one left and it was ordered by Robert, but if he doesn't pick it up by the end of the week it's yours." Suddenly Bill's demeanor completely changed as he calmly replied, "Oh, that's right, I told you guys my name was Robert when I ordered it because I don't like people knowing my real name." After verifying his other contact information, I realized he was telling the truth.

Customer service employees have to deal with a wide range of emotions when trying to serve customers who self-sabotage. It can be frustrating to earnestly attempt to help a customer whose actions make it difficult or even impossible to please them. Customer service gets even more difficult when, despite your best efforts to serve, the self-sabotaging customer assumes the problem is your fault.

This frustration can consume an employee's focus and make it hard to see what they could have done differently or better. They often need a supportive boss or coworker who can help them learn from the situation and come up with different approaches to try the next time they encounter a similar customer. One of my favorite ways to do this is a simple exercise called Expand Your Influence.

To do this exercise with an employee, I first draw a circle on a piece of paper. I explain that everything inside the circle represents what the employee can directly control, and everything outside the circle represents things the employee cannot control. We revisit the difficult situation and list things the employee can control, such as their greeting to the customer. Next, we list things the employee can't control, such as the customer's emotions. Finally, we brainstorm ways the employee can expand their circle of influence to exert greater control on the situation.

I once did the Expand Your Influence exercise with a group of social workers who were frustrated by clients who would show up at their office unannounced and then get upset when their social worker wasn't able to see them. One of the simplest solutions identified during this exercise was to proactively call clients to schedule appointments in advance. This took a few extra minutes of the social workers' time, but they realized they were spending at least that much time dealing with angry clients who showed up unannounced.

Sometimes we just need a way to encourage customers to share more information so we can help them. T-Mobile's social care team does an excellent job of responding to customers who complain on Twitter. A typical response includes a link where customers can share more details about their issue via direct message, which is a private communication channel within Twitter. Representatives also attach cards to their replies with their picture and a short bio as a way to humanize their interactions and make customers feel more comfortable.[20]

The Dishonest Customer

Some customers exaggerate, lie, or even steal. These customers can hurt a business financially, and a common response from management is to implement unfriendly policies that hurt the majority of customers who are honest.

For example, a new sign appeared one day in my local self-serve frozen yogurt shop. It was handwritten and taped to a plastic bin that held small cups used for sampling the yogurt. The sign read:

> *No free samples! Taster cups available for paying customers.*
> *NO sampling after purchase!*

I asked an employee about the new sign and she explained that a few people had helped themselves to free samples without buying anything, so a manager decided to put up the sign. The fear was that too many customers were taking advantage of free samples.

The sign was so unfriendly that it made me question whether or not I wanted to return—even though I only took a sample when trying to decide what flavor to order.

Shoplifting was a constant concern when I worked in a retail clothing store. I've witnessed people grab clothing off the rack and literally walk right out the door. One day, a team of shoplifters stole over 100 pairs of jeans in an instant when a department was temporarily left unattended.

This is an enormous business expense. The reaction is often to implement more security measures, such as alarm tags, locked display cabinets, and restrictions on bringing bags into the store. These are all inconvenient for the average customer who's honest and doesn't intend to steal.

These security measures also put employees in an awkward position, because they can end up spending more time enforcing unpopular rules or unlocking security cabinets than they do helping customers.

Trust is the counterintuitive strategy for handling dishonest customers. The financial gain from trusting customers often far outweighs the expense of a few who steal. For example, the taster cups in the yogurt shop encouraged customers to try new flavor combinations and made for a better experience. Attentive employees added to that experience by making suggestions and engaging customers as they sampled. The extra attention had the added effect of discouraging unreasonable sampling.

Lemonade Insurance has developed a reputation for outstanding service by trusting customers who file a claim. Rather than submit reams of paperwork and wait through a lengthy approval process, customers are able to submit insurance claims via a smartphone app. The company uses an algorithm to quickly assess risk and is able to pay many claims almost instantly as a result. Lemonade approved and paid one customer's claim in just three seconds![21]

The Abusive Customer

Think back to the last time you encountered a total stranger who was rude to you. Perhaps an aggressive driver nearly ran you off the road. Or someone at the grocery store kept bumping their cart into the back of your legs while you were waiting in line. Or you might have met your new neighbor when she started screaming at you from across the street, because she wrongly assumed you weren't picking up after your dog.

Scenarios like these cause your natural defensive instincts to kick in. Your adrenaline levels increase when you're confronted by an aggressive, angry, and unpredictable person. You naturally focus on trying to get yourself out of the situation safely. Afterwards, the memory lingers in a mixture of relief that you're safe and disbelief at the other person's actions.

Now imagine this unpredictable and perhaps angry person is a customer, and it's your job to try to make them happy.

Although not the norm, customers can be abusive. They may yell, scream, rant, rave, and occasionally attack—physically, as well as emotionally. Dealing with them can be a harrowing experience. Here's an example from Andrew, who has worked as a bartender for over 15 years.

I had ten patrons waiting to get a drink, so I had to move quickly, calmly, and deliver the best I could. I finished with one customer, ran his credit card, and set it down in front of him for him to sign. He was talking to the man next to him and I finished with that man, set his credit card down for him to sign. At this point, I was on to the rest of the customers.

One of the two men comes back furious about ten minutes later and blames me for running the wrong credit card. That was not the case; he just thought I did. Apparently he had left with the other man's card instead of his own. The other man was long gone. He begins telling me that I am an idiot and that I need to be fired. He then throws the credit card at my face while demanding that I go out and find the guy who has his credit card.

Needless to say, it worked out in the end. The other guy returned with the credit card later that night and both men got their cards back.

Some customers are so outrageous, their behavior is criminal. Do a Google search on "fast food 911 call" and you'll be treated to story after story of customers calling 911 over customer service disputes. Try Googling "unruly airline passenger," and you'll read stories of angry passengers disrupting flights, some of whose behavior was so bad it prompted concerns about terrorist activity.

Customer service can be tough enough as it is, but abusive customers can make service virtually impossible. The solution to working with these select few customers is simple: invite them to take their business elsewhere.

These customers often represent a net loss for your business after you subtract the cost of discounts, service recovery, and extra employee time from the revenue they bring in. Many of them create an unpleasant scene that negatively impacts other customers and drives them away, too. Perhaps most important, these customers subject your employees to hostile, intimidating, or abusive behavior that can create an environment where your employees don't want to work.

Customer service leaders should expect a lot from their employees, and they should demonstrate a strong commitment in return. When I was a customer service manager, I could tell how grateful my employees were when I calmly and professionally explained to a customer that they couldn't yell and curse at our employees. Sometimes, these customers changed their demeanor after speaking with a manager; other times, they decided to take their business elsewhere. No matter what the result, I always saw my employees renew their commitment to customer service, because they knew I supported them.

Solution Summary: Overcoming Challenging Customers

Understanding the role that customers play in their service experience isn't an excuse for poor employee performance. As you'll see in upcoming chapters, poor customer service can often be attributed to poor employee performance, poor leadership, poor policies and procedures, or all of the above.

However, customer service leaders must understand *all* the reasons why it can be so hard to make customers happy—including the fact that the customer *isn't* always right.

Here's a summary of the solutions presented in this chapter:

- Create generous, customer-friendly policies that make it easier for customers to be right.
- Train employees to avoid placing blame when a customer makes an error, and instead focus on finding a solution.
- Avoid arguing with customers in public forums, such as Twitter, by publicly acknowledging their feelings and offering to address the issue in private.
- Identify new customers and take a moment to let them know what they can expect so they won't encounter any unpleasant surprises.
- Remember that customers tend to hear what they want to hear, so be careful not to be overly optimistic when setting expectations.
- Operate by the Platinum Rule: treat customers the way *they* want to be treated.
- Learn how to get better results with self-sabotaging customers by conducting an Expand Your Influence exercise.
- Trust customers as much as possible to create a more positive experience and prevent unnecessary friction between customers and employees.
- Invite abusive customers to take their business elsewhere to prevent them from draining resources, driving away other customers, and discouraging employees.

CHAPTER 2 NOTES

12   The Quote Investigator website gives a nice overview of the history of "The Customer is Always Right" at https://quoteinvestigator.com/2015/10/06/customer/#note-12180-9. Accessed March 6, 2018.

13   John Goodman. *Strategic Customer Service.* AMACOM. 2009.

14   Edward Baig. "Starbucks letter to employees: No purchases needed to sit inside, use bathroom." *USA Today.* May 20, 2018.

15   Response from @Nike on Twitter, https://twitter.com/c_bear98/status/1022925822674518016. Accessed July 6, 2018.

16   Scott S. Wiltermuth and Larissa Z. Tiedens. "Incidental anger and the desire to evaluate." *Organizational Behavior and Human Decision Processes.* 2011.

17   The American Customer Satisfaction Index, www.theacsi.org. Accessed July 6, 2018.

18   Megan McArdle. "What's not to love about Trader Joe's?" *Washington Post.* March 30, 2018.

19   Frances Frei and Anne Morriss. *Uncommon Service: How to Win By Putting Customers at the Core of Your Business.* Harvard Business School Publishing. 2012.

20   You can view some of T-Mobile's excellent replies by visiting its Twitter feed: www.twitter.com/tmobile. Accessed July 6, 2018.

21   "Lemonade Sets New World Record." Lemonade Insurance press release. January 5, 2017.

CHAPTER 3

Conformity Is Contagious

● ● ●

Creating a Company Culture that Encourages
Outstanding Customer Service

M y wife, Sally, and I went out to a nice steakhouse one evening to celebrate me wrapping up the filming of one of my training videos.

Sally likes her steak medium (with a warm pink center), while I prefer
mine to be medium rare (with a warm red center). Unfortunately, we could
tell as soon as we cut into our steaks that they were overcooked—Sally's
came out well done and mine was medium well.

Our server came over to check on us and quickly agreed the steaks
were overdone. As we discussed our options, a man we didn't recognize
suddenly walked up to our table and joined in the discussion. Without so
much as an introduction or greeting, he tried to debate whether or not our
steaks were truly overcooked.

Who was this guy?

It turns out he was the restaurant's general manager. His sudden presence and brusque manner turned a helpful, problem-solving conversation
with our server into a contentious one with him. The general manager
finally agreed the steaks were overdone and agreed to have the kitchen

prepare new steaks at our desired temperature. We were worried about our original steaks going to waste, but the manager assured us someone in the kitchen would eat them (we hadn't even taken a bite).

The new steaks soon arrived and we eagerly cut into them. This time, they were undercooked! Sally's was fairly close to medium, but mine was rare with a dark red center. To add insult to injury, there was a small wooden flag sticking out of my steak that read "rare."

This looked like a deliberate act!

Our server came back to check on us and we showed her our steaks. She was clearly embarrassed about my intentionally rare steak, and it seemed to catch her off-guard. She told us she'd asked for my steak to be prepared medium rare and wasn't sure why it had come out rare. Sally decided she was content with her steak, but I sent mine back again.

A kitchen runner brought my steak back a few minutes later with the general manager in tow. To our amazement, he admitted that he had over-rode our server and told the chef to make my steak rare. He explained he didn't agree that my original steak was medium well (even though it was brown throughout with just a hint of pink in the middle), so he ordered my new steak rare thinking that's what I really wanted.

We were incredulous!

The general manager agreed to take the steaks off our bill, even though he continued to argue and defend his actions. Finally, I calmly asked him to leave our table so we could finish our meal.

Our server was polite and friendly at the start of the evening, but the interaction with the general manager seemed to change her demeanor. She didn't come back to check on us or refill our water glasses. And she brought the check as soon as we finished our meal, delivering it to the table without a smile or any additional attempt at recovery.

We expect employees like the restaurant server to be polite and friendly, but that's hard to do when the boss is setting a poor example or even deliberately sabotaging service. Bosses have an outsized impact on an organization's culture.

In this chapter, we'll see how employees are influenced to conform to the organizational culture by their supervisor and their coworkers. We'll explore how social pressure shapes employee behaviors in ways they may not even realize. Along the way, we'll examine how company culture is ultimately a product of our actions rather than a catchy slogan or a set of corporate values. Ultimately, we'll see how a strong culture can either be a major obstacle to outstanding customer service, or a powerful force lifting organizations into the ranks of the customer service elite.

Social Pressure Influences Behavior

Look at the pictures below. Which line is the same length as the one on the left?

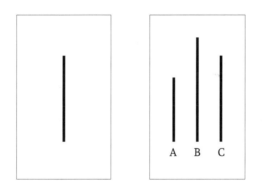

Psychologist Solomon Asch used cards with lines like these to conduct an experiment in 1951. Subjects were told it was a visual acuity test, but it was really an experiment to see if people would conform to social pressure. In the experiment, a subject was placed in a room with several other people and asked to identify the matching line in a series of tests like the one above. Unbeknownst to the subject, the others in the room were actually Asch's assistants and had been instructed to give wrong answers.[22]

The subjects were seated so that they'd be one of the last to respond. All the participants gave their answers out loud, so each person could hear what the others had said. When the assistants all answered incorrectly, the subject also gave the wrong answer 36.8 percent of the time. Some subjects were more independent than others, but nearly 75 percent of them answered incorrectly at least once during the series of tests.[23]

Why did so many people give the wrong answer? Most subjects reported experiencing a conflict between what their eyes told them was the correct response and their desire to avoid contradicting the group. When debriefed after the experiment, they provided a variety of rationales from "I'm wrong, they're right" to "I didn't want to spoil the results of your experiment."

(The correct answer—as you probably identified—is C.)

Asch's experiment revealed that people tend to change their beliefs and actions out of a desire to conform to the norms of a group. In a customer service setting, these group norms are an important part of the company culture. Therefore, if the negative influence of the company culture is strong enough, an employee might knowingly provide poor customer service.

Here's a real-life example. Camille was a guest service associate in a hotel that struggled to serve its customers. She had the natural instincts to be good at customer service, but found herself increasingly frustrated by her coworkers' apathetic attitudes toward guests. She soon found herself falling in line and delivering poor service herself. Giving less than her all in customer service situations bothered Camille, but her desire to avoid the discomfort of standing out from her coworkers was a stronger influence.

Camille eventually left this position to work as a guest service associate in another hotel. Unlike her last job, this hotel had a culture that valued customer service. Camille found encouragement through her coworkers, who all seemed to care deeply about doing their best to make guests happy. She felt relieved that she could use her customer service skills without feeling like an outcast amongst her peers.

Organizational or group culture can even influence our behavior when we're not aware of it.

In a 1935 experiment, psychologist Muzafer Sherif placed subjects in a darkened room, and then turned on a tiny light at the far end of the room. In this situation, a phenomenon called the *autokinetic effect* causes us to perceive that the light is moving, even though it's not. Subjects in the experiment, all unaware of the autokinetic effect, were asked to estimate how far the light moved.

Some subjects were placed in the room by themselves, and their estimates ranged from a quarter inch to 15 inches. Other subjects were seated in the room with two additional participants and asked to give their estimates aloud. This time, the group's estimates quickly converged to a group norm.

Sherif made two interesting discoveries about the groups in this experiment. First, most of the participants were unaware that the other members of the group had any influence on their perception of how far the light moved. They simply believed they were all giving reasonably accurate readings. Second, while there was consensus within the groups, the estimates varied widely between different groups.

These findings show that group norms readily influence our perceptions, yet how we're influenced depends on the dynamics of the particular group.[24] In a customer service setting, employees may not realize they're delivering mediocre or even poor service if they work in an environment where that's the norm. It may require moving to a new organization for them to realize there are other ways to serve.

Sometimes, even moving to a new organization can take some adjustment.

The USS Midway Museum is a decommissioned aircraft carrier that's been rated by TripAdvisor as the top tourist attraction in San Diego, California.[25] Liane Morton, the museum's director of human resources, told me she asks job applicants what they're looking for in a workplace culture.

"A lot of people don't know the answer," says Morton. "They're usually more interested in what their job duties will be and what they'll get paid."

Once employees are hired, a lot of time is spent helping people understand the Midway's unique service culture. "We have a section in our orientation where we make the case for our culture and spend time proving how our culture makes us successful," says Morton. "We share a lot of stories and examples because that really helps people understand our culture better."

Despite careful hiring and training, employees sometimes struggle to unlearn bad habits they learned at previous jobs. Morton explains it can take a lot of coaching to help employees understand that policies are general guidelines, and they're empowered to bend the rules a bit to keep customers happy. "I think it's because they would get in trouble at their last job if they didn't follow the policy precisely," explains Morton.

Most employees aren't inherently good or bad at customer service. Their performance in any particular job can be hugely influenced by the culture that surrounds them. Lousy service might simply be a product of social pressure encouraging employees to treat customers poorly.

Negative social pressure often comes directly from supervisors, as in the example of the steakhouse general manager.

Not long ago, I noticed a declining service level at one of my favorite bakeries. The reason became clear when I heard the supervisor loudly chastising her employees for a missed order. As a customer, I felt uncomfortable witnessing this tirade, and I can only imagine how the employees felt as they were dressed down in front of several customers. There wasn't a smile to be seen on their faces as they went back to work.

This supervisor's rude approach created a great deal of negative pressure that caused her employees to perform poorly. They were clearly tentative in an effort to avoid her continued wrath, which made them less proactive and caused them to work more slowly. Her embarrassing public admonishment sent the message that it was okay to behave rudely in front of customers, and her employees quickly adopted a sullen attitude devoid of any enthusiasm.

Of course, negative social pressure can also come from coworkers. I once facilitated a workshop where the two most experienced employees were also the loudest detractors. Nothing I suggested met with their approval, and their negative outlook suppressed the other participants' willingness to engage in the training. Their supervisor was also attending the training, but he was too meek to stand up to these two curmudgeonly men.

We finally took a break to clear the air. When it was time to return, everyone made it back on time except for the two negative employees. The supervisor hesitantly asked the group if they thought we should wait until they returned before resuming and was answered with a loud chorus of "No!" The rest of the class featured lively discussions and enthusiastic participation, and I breathed a sigh of relief when my two detractors never rematerialized.

Companies must simultaneously create positive social pressure while removing negative influences if they want their employees to provide outstanding service. Some of these solutions will be covered in subsequent chapters; here's a brief summary.

- Make time to catch employees providing good service and recognize their performance so the employee will be likely to repeat it (Chapter 4).
- Avoid policies that may anger customers and cause them to pressure your employees to perform poorly (Chapter 5).
- Fix operational issues that contribute to customer service failures and frustrate employees (Chapter 6).

Another important way to create positive social pressure is for supervisors to act as role models for their employees. My first boss, Christie, was a master at reinforcing a positive customer service culture at the retail clothing store where I worked in high school. She spent a lot of time on the sales floor demonstrating the right way to treat customers through her own terrific customer service. She'd frequently spot an associate doing something great and praise them for their efforts. Christie was also quick to get someone back on track if they didn't provide great service, though this didn't happen very often. She would even thank her employees for a great job at the end of each shift.

Christie's strong and consistent presence made it difficult for anyone to provide anything less than outstanding customer service. I always felt I'd be letting her and my coworkers down if I didn't provide the best service I possibly could. The pressure to conform—in a good way—was always there.

One of the most difficult challenges for any supervisor is working with persistently negative employees. Left unchecked, they'll spread their negative outlook to everyone else on the team. A supervisor must act decisively with these employees to help them adopt a more positive approach to customer service, or else remove them from the team altogether.

A typical approach to managing employee performance is to pinpoint undesirable behaviors or results and get the employee to make a change. Consistently negative employees can be a real challenge to manage, because gaining their agreement on what constitutes a bad attitude is usually difficult. Progressive discipline is hard to use in these situations, because supervisors are often required to provide specific facts and examples when disciplining an employee. Saying someone has a "bad attitude" isn't enough to satisfy that requirement.

When I was a young and inexperienced supervisor, I sat down to counsel a veteran employee about her poor attitude. She responded by simply saying, "I don't have a bad attitude." I tried to back up my assertion with examples, but she countered each one by pointing out she didn't feel she was being negative in those situations. I quickly realized I was in over my head.

Fortunately, I had access to a good mentor who helped me regroup and think about why I thought this employee had a bad attitude. My mentor encouraged me to look for objective data that was hard to refute. One of the key facts that emerged was that I'd received five separate complaints from other department leaders who felt my employee was difficult to work with.

I reapproached my employee and this time focused on the complaints. I told her she didn't have to agree with her colleagues' impressions of her, but it was important that she take steps to ensure the complaints didn't continue. Taking a more positive tone this time, I told her I wanted to see her succeed and offered to brainstorm ways she might convince people in other departments that she was easy to work with.

This second conversation went well. The feedback was difficult for her to take, but it was factual and, more important, actionable. My negative employee agreed to make changes and, over the course of the next few weeks, succeeded in changing quite a few people's minds about her. Over time, she became a reliable employee who worked well with other departments.

Unfortunately, some employees simply refuse to change. When this is the case, customer service leaders need to act decisively to remove those individuals from the team. Losing a disgruntled employee can be like a breath of fresh air, reinvigorating the rest of the team. On the other hand, letting a negative employee stay too long can cause others to yield to that person's influence, and the team in general may lose respect for their supervisor's authority.

Culture Is What We Do

I go to In-N-Out Burger a lot.

The law of averages suggests I should have had a bad experience at least once by now. Some visits have been better than others, but I've never had a bad experience. Not one.

I'm not alone in my admiration of In-N-Out. They're consistently ranked among the top fast food chains in customer satisfaction.[26] The chain only has locations in a handful of states, but people all over the country—and even outside the United States—have become fans, with some devoted followers actually planning a business trip or vacation itinerary around a visit to an In-N-Out.

What's the secret to In-N-Out's success? It may be easier to understand if you compare them to a similar restaurant that struggles with customer service: McDonald's.[27]

The two have a lot in common. While McDonald's has a more diverse menu, both are fundamentally fast food burger joints. Both were founded in Southern California in 1948. Many fast food service concepts in use today originated at either In-N-Out or McDonald's. The two companies even use the same three words as a foundation of their operating principles: quality, service, and cleanliness.[28]

So why is customer service at these two restaurants so different? In a word, culture. Culture defines everything these organizations do when it comes to customer service.

In-N-Out founder Harry Snyder made sure the principles of "Quality, Service, and Cleanliness" were more than just platitudes. He instilled them in everything the company did—and these principles are still present in everything In-N-Out does today. The food is fresh, not frozen. Its stores are clean, even during busy times. Employees are friendly and well-trained. In-N-Out has maintained its remarkable consistency by steadfastly refusing to franchise stores and resisting the urge to expand too quickly.

Culture also shapes many of In-N-Out's business practices, including how the company hires employees. Management believes high-caliber employees are necessary to provide the service and quality they know customers expect. The company offers better wages and working conditions than competitors, which contributes to one of the lowest employee turnover rates in the fast food industry.[29] In 2018, In-N-Out was ranked #4 on Glassdoor's best places to work list, with an overall rating of 4.4 stars out of 5.[30]

When Ray Kroc purchased the McDonald's concept from the Mc-Donald brothers, he talked about those same three words that define In-N-Out's culture. According to the McDonald's website, Kroc once said, "If I had a brick for every time I've repeated the phrase Quality, Service, Cleanliness, and Value, I think I'd probably be able to bridge the Atlantic Ocean with them."[31]

In reality, Kroc's true focus was on rapidly expanding the business. The words quality, service, and cleanliness were clearly less important than a growth strategy based on volume, cost control, and franchising. For example, until as recently as 2018, McDonald's used only frozen burger patties cooked using a special clam-shell grill that cooked both sides of the patty at once to save time.[32]

While franchising allowed McDonald's to grow into a global giant, it's also made it difficult for the company to control the quality of service delivered at its restaurants. Today, approximately 90 percent of their restaurants are run by franchisees, while only 10 percent are run by McDonald's.[33] This means the service customers receive from most of its establishments is largely determined by the management skills and customer service philosophy of an independent franchise owner, rather than by the McDonald's organization.

Culture isn't exclusively defined by an entire organization. As we learned in Chapter 1, different locations within the same company can have varying levels of service. Even at McDonald's, stores with managers good at engaging employees and motivating them to deliver outstanding service typically bring in 10 percent more revenue per year than the average.[34]

When you look at the companies most admired for their customer service, you'll discover that many of them freely share their secrets. Executives give presentations at conferences and frequently grant interviews to various media outlets. Many of these companies are extensively profiled in books and magazine articles. Some, like Disney, share their culture-building process through corporate training programs that anyone can pay to attend.

If a customer-focused culture is so important, and information on how to create one is so widely available, why don't more companies have one? The short answer is that creating a customer-focused culture takes real dedication. Companies that just go through the motions tend to fall short.

Some companies hire ad agencies to develop clever marketing messages that highlight outstanding customer experiences. Defunct electronics retailer Circuit City was once famous for its slogan, "Welcome to Circuit City, where service is state of the art." However, its service was definitely *not* state of the art when the company filed for bankruptcy in 2008. That year, its customer service was ranked second to last for specialty retail stores by the American Customer Satisfaction Index.[35]

Ironically, many of the reasons for Circuit City's undoing were related to strategic decisions that resulted in poor customer service. For example, the company implemented a 15 percent restocking fee on returned products. The decision to impose this fee stemmed from a belief that many customers wanted to buy items, use them, and then return them for a refund. But the fee was widely criticized and even underwent legal scrutiny.[36]

In another highly-publicized example, Circuit City fired thousands of its most experienced and knowledgeable retail associates and replaced them with lower-paid employees. This saved the company some money in the short term, but it also sent the message that the company regarded employees as commodities, rather than a source of competitive advantage.[37]

Some business leaders think it's enough to create lofty customer service platitudes at executive retreats. One company spent a great deal of time and money creating a set of five customer service values that it rolled out to all employees. The company then hired me to determine how well employees understood the new values.

I started by surveying employees throughout the company to test their recollection of the customer service values. A whopping 95 percent of the employees could recite all five values from memory. The remaining

5 percent got four out of five correct. So far, so good.

Next, I asked employees to tell me what the values meant. Here there was near-universal disagreement. Even the CEO, the CFO, and the Vice President of Operations had different definitions! They'd spent so much time coming up with the perfect words that they hadn't stopped to ensure they all understood the same meaning.

Finally, I asked employees how the five customer service values influenced their daily activities. Quite a few felt the service values were a slogan that didn't reflect the true culture. Even more disturbing was a widespread belief that the company's executives failed to consistently align their own decisions and actions with the values. The feeling among many employees was, "Our CEO doesn't really believe in these customer service values, so why should I?"

Some companies have tried to institutionalize a customer-focused culture by including it in formal training programs or an orientation video. This is an admirable step, but two factors can quickly cancel it out if there's no real commitment.

First, the institutional culture message is often delivered by someone other than an employee's direct supervisor. New hires learn about company culture in new employee orientation from a special training class delivered by a corporate trainer, or perhaps a slick video created by the marketing department. However, the employee's supervisor also needs to understand and believe in the company culture. If the supervisor doesn't model the same message, the employee will almost always follow the supervisor's lead, since the boss has direct control over the employee's performance.

Second, most of what employees learn comes from informal rather than formal training. This includes on-the-job training, sharing with coworkers, taking direction from supervisors, reading policies and procedures, and learning from experience. If there's a conflict between the cultural message delivered in formal training and the cultural message learned informally, the latter wins.

Developing a strong customer-focused culture requires an ongoing commitment and dedication, but organizations repeatedly try to find shortcuts that ultimately result in failure. They hold team-building events or invent a catchy slogan to get everyone fired up about service. Unfortunately, these high-energy events often represent the extent of the initiative.

One retailer devoted an entire four-day leadership conference to using customer service to set itself apart from the competition and drive sales. The energy from the group was unbelievable throughout the event. They cheered and applauded each other's presentations. Whenever someone gave the signal, everyone would stand and loudly chant the company's new customer service principles like they were at a giant pep rally before a big game. Participants even had noise makers and confetti to throw around the room, which contributed to the festive atmosphere.

Inevitably, these leaders had to come back down to earth after their conference. When reality set in and they went back to their various locations, they were confronted with a mountain of new tasks, initiatives, and directives. All this new work—and the steady pull of ingrained habits—did more to shape their performance than any good intentions they took away from the leadership conference. Sadly, the company announced massive layoffs a few months later, as they were unable to meet their service or profit goals.

Culture is what we actually do. It can't be created by a marketing campaign, a vision statement, a training program, or a motivational conference. Creating a customer-focused culture takes time, commitment, and perseverance. Most important, it's a never-ending process.

I provide a step-by-step guide for creating a customer-focused culture in *The Service Culture Handbook*, but here's a broad overview of the three principal steps.

The first step is to clearly define the culture by writing what's called a customer service vision. This gives employees clear direction, so they know precisely how they can contribute. The three hallmarks of a strong customer service vision are:

1. It's simple and easily understood.
2. It's focused on customers.
3. It reflects both who you are now and who you aspire to be in the future.

In-N-Out Burger is a great example of a company with a clearly defined customer service philosophy written in plain English:

> "Give customers the freshest, highest quality foods you can buy and provide them with friendly service in a sparkling clean environment."[38]

This philosophy is immediately apparent when you walk into any In-N-Out restaurant. Look into their open kitchen, and you'll see fresh produce or an employee using a slicer to cut whole potatoes into fries. You'll be greeted by a cheerful employee who makes eye contact, smiles, and thanks you sincerely. You'll notice how clean the restaurant is, even if you happen to go during a busy time when the dining area is full of customers. Finally, your experience all comes together when you sit down and take a bite of one of their delicious cheeseburgers.

The second step in creating a customer-focused culture is to engage employees. An engaged employee understands the customer service vision and is committed to helping the organization achieve it.

One way to engage employees is by ensuring everyone can give consistent answers to three questions:

1. What is the customer service vision?
2. What does it mean?
3. How do I personally contribute?

At the USS Midway Museum, employees are incredibly connected to the organization's customer service vision, which also serves as its mission statement:

> *Preserve the historic USS Midway and the legacy of those who serve; Inspire and Educate future generations; and Entertain our museum guests.*

You can see this vision in action when you visit the Midway. It starts with a cheerful greeting from a knowledgeable employee as you buy your ticket. Once on board the ship, helpful employees outfit you with an audio player, allowing you to hear the museum's self-guided audio tour. Perhaps the best part of the experience is the volunteer docents stationed throughout the ship who tell stories about what it was like to live and serve aboard the carrier, with many of the stories coming from firsthand experience.

The third step toward creating a customer-focused culture is for leaders and managers to recognize and act upon the moments of truth that truly define a culture. A moment of truth refers to the myriad of daily decisions a customer service leader must make. This includes setting goals, hiring, training, employee empowerment, and supervision. A company can only claim to have a truly customer-focused culture when the vast majority of its leaders' decisions align with the company's definition of outstanding service.

My local plumbing company is an example of an organization that's developed a reputation for outstanding service by mastering the moments of truth. Plumbers generally have a reputation of showing up late, creating a big mess, and charging enormous fees. Ideal Plumbing, Heating, Air, and Electrical has done the opposite by making customer service a priority in everything they do.

For Don Teemsma, Ideal's President, the hiring process represents the first moment of truth. According to Don, every technician they hire must have both outstanding technical *and* customer service skills. Each candidate is carefully screened and interviewed by at least one manager and one coworker, and any interviewer has the authority to reject a candidate they feel wouldn't live up to Ideal's high standards.

Hiring great people is just the beginning. Don and his management team consistently reinforce the company's customer service philosophy in training, regular team meetings, and daily one-on-one interaction with employees. Don spends a good part of each day checking in on customers at the job site or over the phone to make sure things are going smoothly. From a customer's perspective, Ideal's consistent focus on the moments of truth results in an extraordinarily high level of service.

Creating a customer-focused culture isn't easy. It can take a long time and requires full commitment from leadership. Many organizational leaders start a culture initiative only to be sidetracked by something else.

Gopher Sport, a company that sells sports equipment to schools for physical education and athletic programs, provides a great example of making a true commitment to culture.

"Our CEO established the service vision about five years ago," says Beth Gauthier-Jenkin, the company's Vice President of Customer Care. "The vision is to 'be the easiest company to do business with.' As a company, we often use it in day-to-day conversations as we're making decisions, asking each other: 'Does this direction, decision, etc., make us the easiest company to do business with?' Sometimes the answer is 'no,' and we have to rethink our plans."

Despite a continuous focus on service, there are occasions when an employee will stop embracing the service culture. Gauthier-Jenkin recognizes the impact unhappy employees can have on their coworkers and customers. "Whatever is happening in our contact center, we push that out to our customers. So happy employees equal happy customers while unhappy, miserable employees equal unhappy customers."

She and her management team work with an unhappy employee to help them rediscover their commitment to service, but there sometimes comes a point where the person clearly does not fit the culture. "Whenever you make a very intentional decision to operate based on your culture, you run the risk of losing some people who don't want to be a part of it."

Solution Summary:
How to Create a Customer-Focused Culture

Employees are powerfully influenced by their workplace culture. Delivering outstanding service requires organizations to develop a positive, customer-focused culture, but this can take more hard work, discipline, and dedication than many organizations realize. Here's a summary of the solutions discussed in this chapter:

- Ensure customer service leaders act as role models who actively demonstrate a positive, customer-focused attitude and encourage their employees to do the same.
- Work closely with persistently negative employees to help them change their behavior, and remove them from the team if they're unwilling or unable to improve. If left unchecked, these employees are detrimental to both customer service and team morale.
- Create a clear definition of your customer service philosophy, called a customer service vision, so employees have direction on how to serve customers.
- Engage employees by helping them understand the customer service vision and how they contribute to it.
- Ensure that leadership decisions are consistently aligned with the customer service vision.

CHAPTER 3 NOTES

22   S.E. Asch. "Opinions and social pressure." *Scientific American*, 193, pgs 31–35. 1955.

23   Kenda Cherry. "The Asch Conformity Experiments." Psychology.about.com.

24   Muzafer Sherif. "A study of some social factors in perception." *Archives of Psychology*, Vol. 27, No. 187. 1935.

25   According to www.tripadvisor.com. Accessed September 10, 2018.

26   "New Study from Market Force Information Reveals America's Favorite Quick-Service Restaurants," Market Force press release. April 25, 2018.

27   McDonald's was ranked last in the 2018 American Customer Satisfaction Index for limited service restaurants. In-N-Out is a regional restaurant chain and was not included in the rankings. www.theacsi.org.

28   You can read more about each company's history on their respective websites: www.in-n-out.com and www.aboutmcdonalds.com.

29   Stacy Perman. *In-N-Out Burger: A behind the counter look at the fast food chain that breaks all the rules.* Collins Business, New York. 2009.

30   "Best Places to Work 2018." www.glassdoor.com. Accessed July 22, 2018.

31   McDonald's website, www.mcdonalds.com. Accessed July 22, 2018.

32   https://www.mcdonalds.com. Accessed September 10, 2018.

33   https://www.mcdonalds.com. Accessed September 10, 2018.

34   Lauren Young. "McDonald's Supersized Retirement Plan." *BusinessWeek*. January 12, 2009.

35   www.theacsi.org.

36   Thomas J. Lueck. "Consumer Chief Lambastes Circuit City Return Policy." *New York Times*. December 27, 1997.

37   Anita Hamilton. "Why Circuit City Busted, While Best Buy Boomed." *Time Business*. www.time.com. November 11, 2008.

38   www.in-n-out.com.

CHAPTER 4

They're Your Customers, Not Mine

. . .

Aligning Employees' Interests with Those of the Company

The phone message wasn't good news. The caller was reminding me that my new grill would be delivered that morning. The problem was that I'd scheduled an afternoon delivery. My wife had even arranged to leave work early so she could be home when the grill arrived, but nobody would be there if they came in the morning.

I called back to see if the delivery schedule could be corrected and got an employee named Chris on the phone. I calmly explained that the grill was scheduled to be delivered that afternoon, not that morning.

"Who told you that?"

Ah, four of the worst words to say to an irritated customer. Chris had an opportunity to fix the problem, but instead, he focused on laying the blame somewhere else. He accused the store associate who had sold the grill of getting the delivery schedule wrong. Chris tried to further distance himself from the error by explaining that deliveries were handled by a separate department that only made deliveries where and when it was told by the store.

None of this information mattered to me, and I didn't care whose fault it was. My goal was getting my grill delivered in time for a cookout I had planned that weekend, and sparing my wife the hassle of needlessly taking time off from work. Chris was unable or unwilling to honor the original delivery schedule, so it ultimately took quite a bit of back-and-forth to reschedule the delivery for another date when I knew I would be home all day.

Customer service problems often occur because an employee fails to take ownership of a situation. In this chapter, we'll explore reasons why employees don't necessarily share their employers' customer service goals. We'll also examine how efforts to direct employee behavior—such as providing financial incentives, employee recognition programs, or establishing customer service standards—can often result in unintended consequences. Customer service leaders need to know how to avoid these pitfalls if they want to motivate their employees to serve customers at the highest level.

The Principal-Agent Problem

Customers usually view employees as representatives of the entire company, but employees often see themselves as individuals who are separate from their employer.

I was frustrated with my experience getting my new grill delivered, and Chris was a part of that poor experience. It didn't matter to me that someone in one department sold the grill and someone in another department delivered it. As far as I was concerned, they were all employees of the same company. The salesperson who sold me the grill had agreed on a delivery date and time, and I expected Chris to honor that agreement.

Chris obviously saw things differently. His insistence on identifying a culprit for the scheduling mishap indicated he wasn't consciously responding as a representative of his company. He was acting as an individual whose day just got more challenging because another employee didn't schedule a grill delivery correctly.

Economists refer to the relationship between companies and their employees as the "principal-agent problem." A company (the "principal") hires employees (the "agents") to perform work on behalf of the company. The employees will ideally represent their employer's best interests, but of course, they're also people who have their own motivations.

The principal-agent, or employer-employee, relationship has two primary challenges.[39] First, the goals of the employer and employee can come into conflict. Second, employees operate with a certain degree of autonomy, since the employer can't monitor and control all their actions. This autonomy can make it tempting for an employee to pursue their own self-interest, even if it comes at the expense of their employer.

Both of these challenges were evident during my conversation with Chris. It was in the company's best interests for him to take ownership of the problem and make sure my grill got delivered so they could keep me as a happy customer, but Chris seemed motivated by a desire to avoid blame. He was acting autonomously by attempting to disassociate himself from the problem and the other department, rather than act on behalf of his employer and provide a solution.

It's not hard to find other examples where employees autonomously pursue their own goals instead of their employers'. An employee who takes a cigarette break in front of the store's entrance may look unsightly to customers, but it saves them from spending half their break time walking to and from the designated smoking area behind the store. A retail sales associate might carry on a conversation with a coworker to avoid helping people. A delivery driver may drive like a maniac in the company van, weaving in and out of traffic to get to their destination more quickly, even though they're creating an obvious safety hazard in a vehicle marked with their company's logo.

I once went into a gift shop and discovered that the item I wanted was sold out. When I asked a salesperson to call another location and see if they had what I was looking for, he dialed the number and then handed the phone to me. "Here, you talk to her. I can't stand that lady!" You'd never expect someone to act that way unless you realized his goal was to avoid talking to a coworker he disliked rather than providing me with assistance. The salesperson was also acting autonomously because there wasn't anyone else working in the store to observe or correct his behavior.

This situation reveals another complication in the employer-employee relationship. Employees control information regarding their interactions with customers, so it's unlikely for a supervisor to become aware of an employee providing poor service if they don't observe it directly. Many customers never complain about poor service from employees, and when they do, those complaints often fail to reach a supervisor.

John Goodman estimates that 90 percent of customer complaints are directed to frontline employees.[40] If an employee isn't at fault, you might expect them to take action to resolve the problem or pass the complaint along to someone who can address the issue. But what if handling the complaint isn't in an employee's best interests?

There are several reasons why an employee might not want to address a customer complaint or pass it along to management:

- The employee fears being reprimanded for causing the complaint.
- The employee feels the complaint will not be properly addressed by management, so sharing the information is a waste of time.
- The employee views handling the problem as an annoyance or inconvenience.
- The employee feels they were treated poorly by the customer, so intentionally mishandling the complaint is a means to exact revenge.

To overcome the principal-agent problem, employers need to find a way to align their interests with their employees' personal motivations. This begins with the hiring process. It's not enough to simply hire someone with the right skills to do the job. Companies must hire employees who will love the job and love the company.

The starting point is to make a list of the essential traits or characteristics an employee must have to enjoy working for your company. This list should be the basis of your employee selection process. If you offer a high-energy, fast-paced work environment, then you'll need employees who love that type of work. Someone who prefers a slow and deliberate work style would probably not be a good fit.

A great example is the Renaissance Pleasure Faire, held in Irwindale, California, each April and May. It features Renaissance-themed food, shopping, games, and entertainment. Employees dress in period costumes and stay in character while they work, whether they're a valiant knight, an elegant princess, or a salty merchant.

The Faire is fun in part because the people working there love it! They clearly enjoy the costumes and pageantry. And they like being in character while interacting with guests, many of whom also attend wearing Renaissance-style clothing.

It's also easy to imagine that working at the Faire is not for everyone. There are many people who don't enjoy wearing costumes or who would feel self-conscious about acting in character while serving guests.

Your company may not be quite as unique as the Renaissance Pleasure Faire, but there's likely something special about your organization that sets it apart from others. Think about what some of those characteristics might be. Try talking to your best employees to discover what motivates them to come to work each day. You'll gain insights you can use to search for prospective employees who will also love the job.

Another way to align employee interests with company goals is to involve them with decision-making. Soliciting employee input on designing work procedures, creating customer service strategies, and setting goals helps them gain a sense of ownership. When employees are asked to help write a new policy, they're more likely to understand its importance and meaning—and more likely to follow it.

Involving employees can also convince them to agree to tasks they might otherwise find objectionable. When I worked for a catalog company, our call center representatives were expected to pitch a store credit card offer to certain preapproved customers. Unfortunately, most of our reps had a negative impression of the credit card and felt uncomfortable offering it to customers. As a result, there was a meager 5 percent acceptance rate.

As the call center's training supervisor, I was instructed to devise a training program that would improve our sales performance. The first thing I did was identify a few employees who were highly successful. Some of them got as many as 40 percent of their customers to accept the credit card by enthusiastically promoting several of its features and benefits. It was easy to build a simple training program around the successful formula used by these reps.

When I rolled out the training, I was able to get buy-in from participants by explaining that the techniques they were learning came from their coworkers. I also shared the features and benefits that these employees found got the most positive reactions from customers. Even the most skeptical employees were willing to give the new approach a try once they knew people like themselves had used them. After training thousands of employees over a few months, we increased our average acceptance rate to 20 percent, and many more reps enthusiastically offered the credit card to their customers.

The final piece of the puzzle is an ongoing dialogue between frontline employees and their supervisor. Employees are more likely to develop bad habits or deliver poor service if they aren't properly monitored. Supervisors should regularly observe employee performance and offer praise for good results, while providing constructive feedback when employees stray from the guidelines. This continuous feedback keeps employees aligned with company goals.

This can be challenging for supervisors who find it hard to make time to supervise their employees. They may be overwhelmed with administrative duties, have employees working on several shifts or in different locations, or simply have too many direct reports to pay careful attention to each one. In the big picture, companies must carefully design their supervisors' responsibilities so they have the ability to spend time coaching and developing their employees. At an individual level, supervisors who work hard to encourage good performance soon discover they have to spend much less time correcting mistakes.

Some supervisors find it easy to spot negative performance, but they have a difficult time remembering to recognize and praise an employee for doing something well. Leaders like this may find it helpful to create a simple system to help remind them to spot and encourage positive performance. I know a supervisor who would start each day with five coins in his right pocket. Each time he commended an employee for doing something well, he'd take one of the coins and put it in his left pocket. His goal each day was to move all the coins from the right to the left pocket so that he knew he'd made at least five positive observations.

Customer service levels can improve dramatically when employees and employers share the same interests. Employees are much more likely to follow procedures, adhere to policies, and give extra effort when they are committed to the company's goals. They are also more likely to share rather than suppress valuable customer feedback that can be used for continued improvement.

The Problem with Financial Incentives

Companies often try to solve the principal-agent problem by providing financial incentives for good performance. The assumption is that employees are more likely to act in their employer's best interests if there's money on the line. Unfortunately, financial incentives often cause unintended consequences that can lead to worse—rather than better—service.

Sales commissions are a common form of financial incentive, but they can lead to all sorts of negative results. They may encourage unethical conduct, reduce cooperation between employees, and cause salespeople to focus so much on earning commissions that they ignore other customer service issues. In some extreme cases, sales commissions can lead to fraud or other illegal behavior.[41]

One of the most famous examples occurred in 1992 when Sears, Roebuck and Company was investigated by several state consumer affairs agencies for alleged fraud and deceptive practices in its automotive department. These investigations found that auto mechanics who earned commissions on the revenue they generated consistently recommended unnecessary repairs in an effort to meet sales goals and earn more money. Sears ultimately eliminated sales commissions for its auto mechanics as a result.[42]

Employees who receive tips can help us understand the impact of financial incentives for customer service as well. Many service workers, such as food servers, valet parking attendants, and taxi drivers, depend on tips for a substantial part of their income. However, customer service is only one of several factors that influence the size of a tip. Michael Lynn, a professor at Cornell University's School of Hotel Administration, has conducted extensive research on restaurant tipping and concludes that service quality only influences tipping amounts by an average of two percent.[43]

Social norms and customs provide guidelines for tipping that are generally followed unless a customer receives what they perceive as exceptionally poor or exceptionally good service. Further, since tipping is usually based on a percentage of the bill, a customer who orders a bottle of wine in a restaurant will almost certainly tip more than a customer who orders a soda yet receives the same level of service. There are also individual customers who are particularly cheap or incredibly generous when it comes to tipping, so their unusually small or large tips aren't an accurate reflection of their server's performance.

Like sales commissions, tipping can result in unintended consequences. Some servers may withhold service from a customer they believe will tip poorly. Teamwork may suffer among tipped employees if they believe the extra effort won't result in additional income, and employees might avoid tasks that don't directly result in a tip.

In a perfect world, employees would be intrinsically motived to do their job at a high level without any financial incentives. But sales commissions and tips can be an important part of an employee's income, so it isn't always practical to completely eliminate them. Business leaders who feel they must offer these incentives should carefully design and monitor their use to ensure employees don't have an inadvertent incentive to treat customers poorly.

One best practice is to align financial incentives with team goals rather than individual ones. Notable entrepreneur and *Inc.* magazine columnist Norm Brodsky puts his salespeople on the same bonus system as the rest of his employees rather than a sales-based commission. The result has been a stable sales force that consistently outperforms the competition by working closely as a team and emphasizing long-term customer relationships.[44]

Tipped employees should pool their tips rather than keep everything they individually collect. While this practice may discourage a few of the highest earners, it promotes more teamwork. When I worked for a parking company, valet locations that pooled their tips had consistently higher service levels than locations that did not. One of our locations switched to a tip pooling system and immediately saw valets take a greater interest in activities that impacted service but didn't directly lead to tips, such as greeting arriving vehicles and helping guests unload their luggage.

You see the same effect in restaurants. When tips are shared, servers are more likely to help guests in someone else's section. This team approach raises overall service levels and ultimately increases the tip pool.

Customer service leaders must also monitor employees who receive financial incentives just as closely as they would other employees. Supervisors should never assume that a commission, tip, or bonus provides enough motivation for employees to consistently provide great service.

All service employees need periodic coaching and feedback, regardless of how they are paid.

The Unexpected Side of Rewards and Recognition

Some customer service leaders use reward and recognition programs in lieu of financial incentives as a way of encouraging employees to act in their company's best interests. They offer small rewards for achieving goals or design recognition programs to motivate employees to continue performing at a high level. Unfortunately, even these programs can backfire.

It's important to differentiate between *rewards* and *recognition*.

Rewards are if-then propositions that are designed to incentivize employees to engage in certain behaviors. The actions or results required to earn the reward are spelled out ahead of time so employees know how to win the prize. For example, employees might be told *if* they get mentioned by name in a customer service survey, *then* they will be entered into a drawing for a gift card at the end of the month.

Recognition is given when an employee does something positive as a way of encouraging the employee to repeat the behavior. It can be something tangible—like a gift card or a day off—or something intangible, such as praise from the boss or an employee-of-the-month award. Unlike rewards, the path to earning recognition isn't shared with employees beforehand. It's an unexpected surprise for a job well done.

Of the two, rewards are more likely to cause unwanted behavior, since employees can find themselves focusing on winning the prize rather than serving the customer.

I once walked into a smoothie shop and ordered a smoothie. It was a slow day, and I was the only customer there, along with three employees. One employee took my order and another made my smoothie. As I was leaving the store, the third employee walked up to me and introduced himself. "Hi, I'm Jacob," he said while handing me a card with a survey invitation on it. "We'd really appreciate it if you completed this survey. And please mention me, Jacob!"

It initially struck me as an odd request since Jacob was the only one of the three employees who hadn't served me. So I asked him a few questions and learned that the store had a rewards program where employees could earn prizes if they were mentioned by name in customer service surveys. His entire focus during our interaction was earning a prize rather than creating a better service experience.

So reward programs can create unintended consequences, but employee recognition also has its dangers.

Steve was the parking operations manager for a large sports stadium. One day, he bought donuts for his employees as a way to recognize their hard work and great customer service. The donuts were such a hit that he bought them again before the next game. This soon became a tradition, and Steve brought in dozens of donuts every time there was an event.

Steve's employees were initially delighted by the donuts, but they soon learned to expect them every time. Some employees got discouraged if they didn't get their favorite variety, while others got upset with coworkers who made off with more than their fair share. A few employees even complained that they only received donuts but never bagels or other pastries.

Steve soon discovered that the motivational value of recognition quickly diminishes once it becomes expected—at which point, of course, it's no longer recognition. It began as a special treat, but now his employees would feel something was being taken away from them if he stopped bringing donuts. He summed up the lesson nicely by saying, "Be careful what you start."

Some managers use games, contests, and prizes to promote internal competition and to motivate employees to give extra effort. These also have a hidden trap that can lead to unintended consequences. Employees can easily focus too much of their attention on beating their coworkers and winning the prize, while losing sight of the big picture. I remember a contest like this when I worked at a clothing store as a teenager.

Christie, the store manager, announced one day that the person who helped the most customers over the course of a week could write their own work schedule for the following week. This was a huge prize for me, so I went out of my way to help every customer I could and ended up the winner. Christie ran the contest the next week, and I won again, aided in part by my plum work schedule. She finally discontinued the contest when she realized having one part-time employee (me!) name his own hours created scheduling challenges for all the other employees.

The contest was great for me, but it hurt both customer service and sales because it gave me an incentive to concentrate on behaviors that would help me win. Since the contest was based on the number of customers assisted rather than on total sales, I tried to interact with as many customers as possible. This meant limiting the amount of time I spent with any one person so I could move on to the next one. It also took my attention away from other duties, such as keeping the dressing rooms clean, refolding clothes in my department, and checking stock for people who called the store.

Recognition can be used as an effective employee motivation tool, but it must be unexpected and occur after a desired outcome is achieved. This way, recognition becomes a way of showing appreciation for good work rather than a means of incentivizing behavior.[45] That's why Steve's donuts were so well received the first time, but were soon taken for granted when they became routine.

Unexpected rewards also eliminate the possibility of employees changing their behavior just to win a prize. A client of mine worked diligently to improve customer service survey scores and encouraged every employee to work toward their team goal. It was only after they achieved their objective that my client threw a big party to celebrate their accomplishment. Had they announced the party ahead of time, the employees might have decreased their performance afterwards, since the celebration would feel like the end of a journey. Making the party a surprise motivated employees to continue their performance, since they felt appreciated for what they had accomplished.

Customer Service Standards that Backfire

The industrial era led to the development of management methods that emphasize strict adherence to standard operating procedures. This approach works well in a manufacturing environment where the goal is to produce each widget quickly and to exactly the same specifications. But a series of well-defined processes tends to fall short when applied to relationships between human beings.[46]

My local grocery store once had a policy that required checkers and baggers to ask customers if they'd like assistance carrying their purchases to the car. The standard was put into place to foster a consistent level of service and to make sure customers didn't feel discriminated against when one customer was offered assistance while another wasn't. Unfortunately, this requirement left no room for employees to use their own discretion. I once purchased a single pack of gum and my cashier dutifully asked, "Do you need any help out to your car today?"

Service standards like these place employees' attention on a task (offering assistance) rather than an outcome (customer satisfaction). Employees know they might be monitored by their supervisor or even a secret shopper with a checklist of required actions. Failure to fulfill all the required actions could lead to disciplinary action. On the other hand, employees might receive a small bonus or another form of recognition for maintaining 100 percent compliance with the requirements.

This creates the potential for an employee to receive praise for complying with internal service standards while delivering poor service in the eyes of the customer. Being asked if I needed assistance carrying my pack of gum to the car felt awkward and inauthentic, even though the employee was doing exactly what she was supposed to do.

Contact centers are notorious for requiring their customer service reps to adhere to a long list of standard responses. Many of these calls really are monitored for "quality assurance and training purposes" by a supervisor or quality assurance technician who listens to the call and verifies whether each requirement is met. Unfortunately, these requirements often have little to do with customer satisfaction. A rep who answers the phone using the correct scripted greeting might get points for compliance even if they delivered the greeting in a monotone voice that was completely devoid of warmth and enthusiasm. On the other hand, the rep may be disciplined for failing to upsell, even if their customer specifically says, "I don't want to buy anything else or hear about any other products today."

Some customer service standards may sound terrific in a marketing meeting but fail to resonate when put into practice. I was once shopping in a shoe store and stepped into a short line to wait for a cashier after making my selection. When it was my turn, the cashier called me over by saying, "I can help the next shoe lover over here." That phrase may have been engineered to accurately reflect the company's brand positioning strategy, but it felt forced and a little weird in practice.

Like financial incentives and recognition, customer service standards can lead to unintended negative consequences. A company that provided computer support for its clients routinely included a service level agreement in its contracts. The service level agreement stipulated an average response time for handling trouble tickets submitted by the client.

The service provider's employees quickly found a loophole in the agreement and began closing trouble tickets without verifying that the problem had been corrected. In many cases, the problem hadn't been fixed, so the client had to open a new trouble ticket since the previous one was closed. This created an additional hassle for the client, but the practice helped employees meet the standard for average time to close a ticket.

Companies are right to try to create a consistent customer experience, but the best way to do this is often through broad guidelines rather than rigid standards. Guidelines allow employees to adapt to each individual customer's needs and use their unique personalities to make the service they provide more authentic.

True Value is consistently recognized for its hardware stores that offer outstanding customer service. My local True Value hardware store requires employees to greet customers immediately and offer them assistance. How they do it is up to them, as long as they make the customer feel welcome and the customer finds what they came to buy.

An employee once greeted me by saying, "What are *you* doing in here?" He had helped me several times over the past few days after a home project caused me to make several unexpected trips to the store. Each time, we joked that we hoped this would be the last time I would have to come back in to get supplies for this particular project. This greeting was a fun and friendly way of telling me he hoped my project hadn't sent me back to the store yet again. It put a smile on my face and made me feel welcome.

Solution Summary: Getting Employee Buy-in

Aligning employee motivation with their company's interests can be a challenging task, but it's an essential part of building an organization capable of delivering outstanding customer service. Companies should strive to put employees in a position where their intrinsic motivation leads them to the right action, rather than trying to manipulate employees through incentives that may have negative side effects.

Here is a summary of the solutions presented in this chapter:

- Hire people who will love their job and love your company so they naturally want to do what you ask them to do.
- Involve frontline employees in decision-making and problem-solving so they take ownership of company goals.
- Frequently monitor employee performance so you can recognize

positive achievements and correct mistakes.

- If you must use financial incentives—such as commissions or tips—be sure to align them with team goals rather than individual accomplishments.
- Don't assume that commissioned or tipped employees need less supervision than employees who aren't paid by performance. They require the same monitoring and coaching as anyone.
- Make employee recognition an unexpected event. This shows employees they're appreciated while keeping their focus on customer service rather than earning a prize.
- Use broad service guidelines rather than detailed standards to allow more flexibility and personalization.

CHAPTER 4 NOTES

39   Kathleen M. Eisenhardt. "Agency Theory: An Assessment and Review." *Academy of Management Review*, Vol. 14, No. 1, pgs 57–74. 1989.

40   John Goodman shared this statistic in a presentation called "Treating Employees as Customers" at the ICMI Dreamforce 2010 conference in San Francisco.

41   Lisa D. Ordonez, Maurice E. Schweitzer, Adam D. Galinsky, and Max H. Bazerman. "Goals Gone Wild: The Systematic Side Effects of Over-Prescribing Goal Setting." Harvard Business School, Cambridge, 2009.

42   Lawrence M. Fisher. "Sears Auto Centers Halt Commissions After Flap." *The New York Times*. June 23, 1992.

43   Robert J. Kwortnik Jr., W. Michael Lynn, and William T. Ross Jr. "Buyer Monitoring: A Means to Insure Personalized Service." *Journal of Marketing Research*, American Marketing Association, pgs 573–583. October 2009.

44   Norm Brodsky and Bo Burlingham. *The Knack: How Street-Smart Entrepreneurs Learn to Handle Whatever Comes Up*. Penguin Group, New York, 2008.

45   Daniel Pink. *Drive: The Surprising Truth About What Motivates Us*. Riverhead Books, New York, 2009.

46   John H. Fleming and Jim Asplund. *Human Sigma. Managing the Employee–Customer Encounter*. Gallup Press, New York, 2007.

CHAPTER 5

Your Employees are Double Agents

• • •

Bridging the Gap Between Doing the Right Thing for the
Customer and Following Company Policy

Some customer service situations are frustrating for both the customer and the employee. I had one of these mutually-challenging experiences when I purchased a paper shredder at my local office supply store. The shredder was intended to replace one I'd thought was broken, but after returning home with the new shredder I discovered that the old shredder had stopped working due to user error. (It appears those safety features designed to protect you from shredding your fingers actually do work!) This seemed like a happy discovery until I looked at the receipt and saw it was clearly marked *Exchanges only—no returns.*

This "no shredder returns" policy was apparently an exception to the store's 100 percent satisfaction guarantee that allows you to return an item for a refund within 30 days of purchase. I hadn't removed the new shredder from the box, so I took it back to the store and tried to return it, despite the warning on the receipt. The customer service associate listened to my story and then meekly explained that shredders couldn't be returned.

"Can I get store credit?" I asked. The associate told me they weren't able to provide store credit, even though the shredder was still sealed in its box.

I tried another tactic. "I know this was my mistake, but are there any other options besides being stuck with a shredder I don't want or need?"

This was a no-win situation for the employee. He obviously saw the logic of my argument, but he was under strict instructions not to allow any shredders to be returned. He could violate the store's policy and return the shredder, but then he'd likely get in trouble. He could refuse to return the shredder, but then he'd run the risk of making a customer angry who would probably complain to his boss.

The employee finally offered to get his manager to see what he could do.

I retold my story when the store manager appeared, acknowledged my error, and asked him for his assistance. The manager looked at the unopened box and quickly realized the "no shredder returns" rule wasn't written for my situation. To my surprise and pleasure, he promptly refunded my money.

In this chapter, we'll see how service failures like the one I narrowly avoided can occur when employees are forced to balance the competing needs of their employer and their customers. We'll examine how customer service representatives ultimately make decisions that are in their own best interests when these types of conflicts occur. We'll even look at some surprising research that suggests customer service leaders are more likely to create these sorts of situations when they don't have direct customer contact.

The Double Agent Problem

In Chapter 4, we examined the principal-agent problem, where companies can struggle to get their employees to act on their behalf. Customer service employees can feel like double agents because they serve two principals: their employer and the customer. This means three sets of self-interest are present, and potentially competing, in every customer service interaction[47].

Let's look at the office supply store example and imagine each party's interests in this situation (as summarized in Figure 5.1).

FIGURE 5.1. ONE CUSTOMER SERVICE INTERACTION, THREE SETS OF SELF-INTEREST.

Party	Interests
Store Manager	Sell paper shredders at a reasonable profit. Used shredders cannot be reconditioned and sold as new, so accepting returns hurts profitability.
Store Employee	Do the best job possible. This includes not getting in trouble with the manager *or* making customers angry.
Me	Return the shredder for a refund or store credit. I don't want to get stuck with an expensive shredder I don't need.

Are the three parties' interests incompatible? The store manager's "no returns or exchanges" policy certainly makes it seem that way to the employee. The policy was written because the store can't resell a shredder that's been used, and management wanted to provide employees and customers with clear and unambiguous guidance. But my situation was a gray area that couldn't be easily addressed with a black-and-white policy. The shredder hadn't been removed from the box and could be resold, even though the employee didn't have the authority to make the right decision. He was stuck between the policy and common sense.

Rigid policies that don't allow for employee discretion—even when they become absurd or unfriendly to customers—can lead to a double agent problem. A stadium concession stand may be covering its legal risk by requiring employees to check ID on anyone buying alcohol, but it could be annoying to a 70-year-old customer with gray hair and a wrinkled face who didn't bring their ID when they went to buy a beer. A customer who calls their cable company to discuss a billing issue may not be in the mood to hear the customer service rep make a required sales pitch about premium channels. A store that requires customers to check their bags at the front may deter a few thieves, but could also turn off quite a few customers who feel that they can't be trusted not to steal.

You may recall reading about David Dao in Chapter 1. He was the United Airlines passenger who was physically dragged off a plane to make room for one of the airline's crew members. The United employees involved that day were an extreme example of double agents.

Passengers had already boarded the flight when United's gate agents learned they needed to make room for crew members. Per the airline's policy at the time, gate agents could offer passengers a maximum of $800 as compensation for giving up their seat and accepting another flight. Employees became stuck between a mandate to get crew members to their destination and the common sense idea that paying passengers seated on a plane who posed no security risk were entitled to be on the flight.

Since then, United has changed its policies to give employees an opportunity to avoid these types of situations. Crew members must now be booked at least 60 minutes before departure. Passengers already on board will not be asked to give up their seats involuntarily, and law enforcement won't be called unless there's a safety or security issue. Gate agents are now empowered to offer up to $10,000 to entice passengers to give up their seat in an overbooked situation.[48]

Not every double agent situation is as absurd as the passenger-dragging incident. Many, like my attempt at returning an unused shredder, arise out of a conflict between a policy and common sense.

Employees who feel caught in the middle can make matters worse if they try to remain neutral. Some double agents have even developed their own customer service phrases that highlight their frustration. If you've ever encountered a double agent, you may have heard a few of these phrases:

- "Hey, I don't make the rules."
- "I just do what I'm told to do."
- "You'll have to ask the boss why we do it this way."

Do any of those phrases sound familiar? They're used by employees attempting to disassociate themselves from their company. But, as you may recall from Chapter 4, customers tend to view the company and the customer service representative as one and the same. A double agent employee who tries to remain neutral may come across as lazy or uncaring; rather than engendering sympathy for their dilemma, their comments and behavior have the opposite effect.

Companies offering outstanding customer service avoid creating double agents by eliminating the potential for conflict between their customers and their employees—and that means eliminating the factors that create double agents in the first place. They avoid policies that are obviously unfriendly to their customers. They try to see beyond the value of each individual transaction to understand the value of a happy customer, and they empower their employees to do the same.

Customer service leaders set rigid policies because they worry about customer abuse or employee error. For example, the office supply store manager might worry about losing money if customers return shredders that can't be resold. Giving employees the discretion to determine if merchandise is resalable may not solve this problem in the minds of corporate policy-makers if they don't trust their frontline employees to make good decisions.

You have to speak the language of business to get past this fear, so let's see what happens when we run some numbers on shredder returns.

The average gross margin for retail office supplies is 39.4 percent.[49] That means a $100 shredder costs the store an estimated $60.06 ($100 – [39.4 percent × 100]). By this estimate, the store stands to lose $60.06 if it accepts a returned shredder that can't be resold or returned to the manufacturer. That looks like a sizable loss on one item.

But let's look at the bigger picture. At the time, I was spending an average of $500 per year at this store. This translates to an annual gross profit of $197.50 at a 39.4 percent average gross margin. When we compare that to the potential loss of $60.06 on the shredder return, we see that my average contribution to the office supply store's profitability is more than three times what they'd lose by refunding my money for a shredder that can't be resold.

Now the business case looks a little different. The store could lose $60.06 if they accept the return of a shredder that can't be resold, but they would lose $197.50 *per year* if they refused the return and I decided to take my business to a competitor.

Of course, the store wasn't in danger of losing anything since the shredder I returned was unopened and could easily have been resold. In retrospect, the frontline customer service associate was needlessly put in a double agent position by a bad policy.

L.L.Bean is an example of a company that has built a reputation for outstanding customer service with the help of a generous returns policy. The retailer realizes the key to long-term success is making sure customers are happy with their products and trusting that the majority of their customers won't abuse this generosity. This philosophy helped L.L.Bean earn the #1 ranking on Prosper Insights & Analytics Customer Service Champs list three years in a row.[50]

The company's return policy is clearly posted on its website:

> We stand behind all our products and are confident that they will perform as designed. If you are not 100% satisfied with one of our products, you may return it within one year of purchase for a refund. After one year, we will consider any items for return that are defective due to materials or craftsmanship.[51]

L.L.Bean's return policy means its employees aren't stuck between the customer and the company when a customer is unhappy with a purchase.

According to Dennis, a former L.L. Bean employee, customer service representatives are instructed to make it easy for a customer to return a purchase. "It was never a question about returns. Customers would call to ask how to return something, and I'd just give them the information on how to return it."

Creating policies that some customers won't like is sometimes unavoidable. For example, L.L.Bean once had a lifetime guarantee that allowed customers to return products at any time, no matter how long ago they were purchased. The company announced a new, one-year limit to the unconditional return policy in February 2018, citing the growing cost of customer abuse. Some people were buying old L.L.Bean products at garage sales and returning them for full refund. Others would return items they were completely satisfied with that were simply worn out from years of normal use.[52]

A few customers complained, but most recognized L.L.Bean's policy is still one of the most generous in retail. A customer can buy a new jacket, wear it for an entire winter season, and then return it for a full refund simply because they don't like it. Generous policies like this may cost a little more in the short term, but L.L.Bean is rewarded with legions of loyal customers who buy clothes and equipment from the company year after year.

The bottom line is trust when it comes to avoiding double agent situations. Companies that distrust their customers and employees end up creating rigid policies that cause employees to get stuck between a rock and a hard place. On the other hand, companies that emphasize trust, generosity, and goodwill almost always create more positive and profitable relationships between their employees and customers.

Weighing Risk Versus Reward

When a customer service employee feels caught between their employer and their customer, their actions may be decided by their perception of risk versus reward. On the one hand, they can follow the employer's policies and avoid getting into trouble with their boss, but this risks angering the customer. On the other hand, they can side with the customer and be rewarded with the customer's gratitude, but then they risk getting in trouble for violating the company's policy.

Employees experiencing conflict in double agent situations tend to be influenced by two factors:

1. Whether their actions are monitored.
2. What the consequences are for pleasing or displeasing each principal.

Employees are more likely to side with their employer over the customer if their actions are being monitored and they feel at risk of being reprimanded. Call center employees tend to be sticklers to company policy since most, if not all, of their calls are recorded and have the potential to be reviewed. Employees who work in close proximity to their supervisor know their supervisor may be watching them at any given time. Any transaction that results in an electronic record also increases the chances a double agent employee will side with their company.

Returning the shredder at the office supply store required a transaction that would be captured in the store's computer. Toeing the line and refusing a shredder return makes sense from the employee's perspective, because a refund for a shredder is likely to be noticed. The store's computer may have even required a manager override to approve the transaction, so the employee couldn't do it without the manager's knowledge.

An employee's risk versus reward calculation may change in situations when they are not easily monitored. Employees who work autonomously or whose work is not digitally monitored are less likely to be observed by their supervisor. Double agent employees may be more likely to side with their customers if they feel they won't get caught.

My wife and I often bring our own bottle of wine when dining out.

This is fairly common in California, where many people are wine enthusiasts and liquor laws allow it. Restaurants typically charge a $15 to $25 corkage fee to open and serve the wine, which is usually much less than the markup on wine purchased from the restaurant. The corkage fee ensures the restaurant still makes a nice profit, even though customers aren't buying the wine from them.

Over the years, I've observed that servers waive the corkage fee nearly 10 percent of the time. We don't ask for them to waive the fee; it just doesn't appear on the bill. This is even more likely to happen when we're regular guests at the restaurant and have gotten to know the servers, or when we're dining with a larger group and bring in more than one bottle.

Waiving the fee saves us money, but it costs the restaurant revenue. So why do servers do it?

The decision to waive the corkage fee may come down to the incentives and disincentives that guide a double agent's behavior. Unlike a shredder return at the office supply store, where all returns are tracked electronically, the restaurant's corkage fee is hard to monitor. Since we're bringing in our own bottle, no wine comes out of the restaurant's stock. It's common to enjoy a bottle of wine with dinner, so a bottle at the table doesn't necessarily signal that a corkage fee is in order.

This leads to the second factor that influences an employee's risk versus reward calculation: the consequences involved. Restaurant corkage fees can generate complaints from customers who aren't used to the practice or who feel the fee is too high. On the other hand, waiving the corkage fee is an easy way for our server to give us a little something extra with our meal. There's a good chance we'll be happier with their service and increase the tip correspondingly.

Employees will sometimes engage in unethical or even illegal behavior when their actions are unmonitored and the rewards are great enough. A nightclub bouncer could put the club's liquor license at risk if they let in an underage drinker, but a small bribe might get them to look the other way if a manager isn't watching. These bribes might add up to become a significant source of income and could outweigh any fear of getting caught and losing his job.

Companies can do several things to help their employees make better decisions in situations where their customers' demands seem at odds with the organization's best interests. As discussed earlier in this chapter, the first step is to institute more customer-friendly policies. Employees have less incentive to act on their own when their company's interests are aligned with the customers.

Let's look back at restaurant corkage fees. Many restaurants have reduced this problem by offering "free corkage Wednesdays" or similar promotions. Other restaurants promote local businesses by waiving the corkage fee on wines purchased from local wine shops or wineries in the region. These promotions can entice more customers to dine at the restaurant while avoiding any double agent problems a corkage fee might cause.

Another great example comes from Virgin Hotels. The high price of drinks and snacks sold from in-room minibars are a frequent guest complaint. To keep guests happy and prevent associates from having to handle those complaints, the hotel chain implemented "street pricing" on minibar items. This pricing policy means minibar items are sold for the same price they would at a convenience store down the street.[53]

Careful monitoring is important to give employees less incentive to act on their own. When I worked for a parking management company, we often increased revenue by 30 percent or more when we took over a parking garage from a competitor. Our secret was a rigorous auditing process that discouraged employee theft and ensured customers were charged the appropriate parking fee. People don't like to pay for parking, so complaints are a natural part of the parking business, but employees knew they'd be caught if they gave in to the demands of an unreasonable customer and lowered or dropped the fee.

Training is another way to prevent employees from becoming double agents. There are certain situations, like charging a parking fee, where it may be impossible to align the company's and customer's interests. Employees who have the skills to effectively handle tricky situations are less likely to give in to a customer's unreasonable demands.

One of the best techniques employees can learn is to provide options instead of saying "No." The word "No" can trigger a customer's anger because it makes them feel powerless. Providing options is usually more acceptable, since it invites the customer's cooperation. For example, at the parking company, I trained our attendants to give customers the option of paying the full fee or going back into the building to get their parking validated when applicable. Customers were much less likely to get upset when it was their choice to pay the full fee, rather than spend extra time to save a few dollars with a validation.

Getting Employees to Do the Dirty Work

The television show *Undercover Boss* exposes an interesting bit of workplace psychology: it's easier for bosses to ask an employee to do something unpopular than it is for them do it themselves.

In each episode of the show, an executive dons a disguise so they won't be recognized and goes "undercover" to shadow employees working frontline positions in their own company. The boss's goals for participating in the show usually include seeing if their executive decisions are being carried out on the front lines. During the show, the bosses almost always make surprising discoveries about the quality and consequences of those decisions.

One episode featured Michael Rubin, then CEO of GSI Commerce. GSI Commerce provided marketing, customer service, and order fulfillment services to help companies like Major League Baseball sell merchandise. Rubin found himself squarely in the middle of the double agent problem during a segment where he took customer calls in the escalations department of one of the company's call centers.

An upset customer called because she discovered she was being charged $149 for a $99 item. The customer wanted to pay the correct price, but was told the company policy was to charge her $149 and then issue a $50 credit to fix the error after the item had shipped. Her call had been transferred to the escalations department, and now Rubin had to handle the irate caller.

The undercover CEO struggled. Simple logic dictated that the customer should pay the correct price, but his own company policy didn't allow him to do this. The customer's anger coupled with his inability to do anything about it left him at a loss for words. Danielle, the call center employee he was shadowing, had to step in and take over the call.

Danielle was now facing the double agent dilemma. Unaware that she was sitting next to the company CEO, she resorted to treating the customer rudely. At one point she informed Rubin that the way to handle the customer was to sound confident and "put her in her place."

Unfortunately for Danielle, Rubin was able to step back into the role of CEO when she took over the call from him. His focus shifted from the obvious discomfort of the double agent dilemma to annoyance at how rudely Danielle was treating the customer. Danielle's performance, not the restrictive policy, became the focus of his attention.

Each *Undercover Boss* episode ends with a segment where the employees the boss shadowed are called to the corporate office. Here they discover whom they were actually working with. During this segment, Rubin reprimanded Danielle for her performance and told her he was going to have her retrained. He made no mention of addressing the policy that caused the problem in the first place.

John Hamman, George Loewenstein, and Roberto Weber are social scientists at Carnegie Mellon University who discovered a possible explanation for Rubin's behavior. They conducted an experiment where participants were given $10.00 and instructed to share as much as they'd like with another participant. Next, they were asked to repeat the experiment, but this time they used an intermediary (i.e., an employee) to share the money on their behalf. On average, participants shared $1.00 less when using an intermediary than when they shared the money directly.[54]

The implication of the experiment—and of the *Undercover Boss* segment—is that unfavorable or unethical policies are easier for managers to implement if they don't have to carry them out themselves. Insulated from angry customers and frustrated frontline employees, executives turn to data such as financial statements, cost/benefit analyses, and other tools to make decisions that impact customer service. Executives who are really out of touch might dismiss negative feedback as the viewpoint of a small minority rather than something to be legitimately concerned about.

Bank of America grabbed headlines in September 2011, when they announced they would begin charging customers a $5.00 monthly fee for making purchases with their debit card.[55] Consumer outcry was loud and swift, but CEO Brian Moynihan initially defended the decision as being in the best interests of the company and its shareholders. In an interview with CNBC's Larry Kudlow, Moynihan explained that the fees were an effort by the bank to be transparent and upfront with its customers while maximizing profitability. Moynihan was insistent that the decision to implement the fee was made only after gathering extensive feedback from customers, and he was convinced that customers would accept the fee in the long run.[56]

However, Bank of America faced a wave of criticism from its customers in the month that followed. One customer collected 153,000 signatures on a petition denouncing the fee.[57] The Credit Union National Association released a study that suggested as many as 650,000 customers had transferred their accounts to a credit union in response to fees at Bank of America and other institutions.[58] Protesters even organized a National Bank Transfer Day to encourage people to move their accounts in response to new bank fees.

Moynihan was undoubtedly aware of the bad press, and he repeatedly had to answer questions about the $5.00 fee as he made the rounds on the talk show circuit. What he didn't have to do was spend his day working face-to-face with the bank's angry customers. That was left to the tellers, the contact center representatives, and other employees who were on the frontlines of customer service.

Ultimately, Bank of America relented to the growing pressure and dropped its plans to implement the $5.00 fee. In an interview published in *The Boston Globe*, Moynihan admitted the fee was a mistake. "We didn't do our best work there. We did a lot of testing, but the customer spoke and we pulled it back."[59]

My own bank, a Bank of America competitor, also raised fees in 2011 that drove customers to other banks. Customer after customer came in to close their account or complain about the new fees, and this constant criticism began to wear on the bank's frontline employees. Several employees told me they felt frustrated and powerless, because the bank's executives had decided to impose fees, but they were the ones who had to field the complaints, try to justify the decision, and make what was often a futile attempt to retain the customer's business.

The solution to avoid being insulated from customers is quite simple. Executives must spend time on the front lines to see what's really going on in their operation. They should listen directly to customers and frontline employees so that their decision-making is influenced by real feedback and not just aggregate numbers on a spreadsheet or a slick presentation from the marketing department. They should observe their operations to see if employees are truly delivering the kind of service they expect their customers to receive. And they should take time to carefully explain strategic decisions and policy changes so employees have an opportunity to understand and embrace their leader's vision.

This leadership approach is sometimes referred to as "management by walking around," and has been practiced by many legendary customer service leaders. Walt Disney, Bill Marriott, and In-N-Out founder Harry Snyder were all famous for their willingness to view their businesses from the ground level to understand what was really happening. William Rosenberg, the founder of the Dunkin Donuts franchise, tirelessly visited his franchisees to ensure their food quality and customer service met his exacting standards. He was even known to dump out a batch of coffee when he visited a Dunkin Donuts store if the coffee wasn't fresh enough.[60]

In her book *What Great Brands Do*, brand leadership expert Denise Lee Yohn tells the story of a group of fast food restaurant executives who were out of touch with their customers' experience. Yohn gave them an assignment to visit restaurants at various times of day and bring a friend to get an outsider perspective. According to Yohn, "The final step was to visit the restroom at a restaurant and sit on the toilet to get a truly authentic experience of the facilities." The exercise helped the executives quickly realize the chain's restaurants were dirty and unkempt.[61]

Solution Summary: Avoiding the Creation of Double Agents

The double agent problem comes from a conflict between the company and the customer, with the employee stuck in the middle. The ultimate solution for any company trying to provide outstanding customer service is to identify these harmful pressures and neutralize them as much as possible. It should be easy and natural for an employee to *want* to do the right thing for both the customer and the company.

Here's a short summary of specific ways to help employees avoid becoming double agents:

- Avoid policies that are certain to anger customers and require your employees to face customer displeasure.
- Whenever possible, allow employees to use their discretion when carrying out corporate policies; this gives them the flexibility to meet the needs of both the company and the customer.
- Find ways to offer the customer choices instead of a flat "No."

- Look beyond a single transaction to consider the lifetime value of a customer when setting restrictive policies or implementing new fees.
- Trust that the vast majority of your employees and customers are not trying to take advantage of you.
- Make sure employees are adequately monitored so you can guide their performance.
- Identify and eliminate incentives that may cause employees to act against the company's best interests.
- Spend considerable time interacting with employees and customers to avoid becoming insulated from reality when making policy decisions.

CHAPTER 5 NOTES

47   Susan R. Ellis, Siegfried P. Gudergan, and Lester W. Johnson. "The Satisfaction Mirror as a Principal-Agent Problem." ANZMAC Conference, 2000.

48   Jon Ostrower. "The 10 things United is doing to avoid another dust-up, drag-out passenger fiasco." CNNMoney.com. April 27, 2017.

49   Source: The retail owner's institute, www.retailowner.com. Accessed July 14, 2018.

50   "Customer Service Champions: L.L.Bean Gets Top Honors, Edges out Amazon for Third Year in a Row." Prosper Insights and Analytics press release. July 24, 2017.

51   Source: www.llbean.com. Accessed September 17, 2018.

52   Shawn Gorman. "A Letter to Our Customers." L.L.Bean Facebook page, https://www.facebook.com/llbean/posts/10155636619902415. February 9, 2018.

53   Joe Sharkey. "Virgin Hotels bucks trend, won't have extra fees." *The New York Times.* November 27, 2017.

54   John R. Hamman, George Loewenstein, and Roberto A. Weber. "Self-interest through delegation: An additional rationale for the principal-agent relationship." Carnegie Mellon University, Pittsburgh, PA. 2009.

55   Blake Ellis. "Bank of America to charge $5 monthly debit card fee." CNNMoney.com. September 29, 2011.

56   Jennifer Liberto. "BofA chief: We have a 'right to make a profit'." CNNMoney.com. October 5, 2011.

57   Devin Dwyer. "Bank of America Customer Delivers 153,000 Signatures in Petition Over Fee." ABC News blogs. October 6, 2011.

58   Credit Union National Association press release. November 4, 2011.

59   Todd Wallack and Shirley Leung. "Moynihan: 'Our job is to be fair to consumers'." *The Boston Globe*. December 21, 2011.

60   William Rosenberg and Jessica Brilliant Keener. *Time to Make the Donuts*. Lebhar-Freedman Books, New York, 2001.

61   Denise Lee Yohn. *What Great Brands Do*. Jossey-Bass, San Francisco, 2013.

Mutually Assured Dissatisfaction

● ● ●

Getting Beyond Broken Systems that
Cause Employee Disengagement

It's never a good sign when a customer service representative uses the word *they* to refer to their own company. It indicates the employee is disassociating themselves from their employer and often means you're about to receive poor service.

When I had to ship my malfunctioning laptop back to the manufacturer so it could be repaired under warranty, it was frustrating enough to lose the use of a new computer. My laptop was expected to be returned within three days, but then I received an email from the company telling me a part that was needed to make the repair was on backorder. Even worse, the repairs department didn't know when the backordered part would arrive.

I called the customer service line, and a representative named Sherry answered the phone. She was polite, friendly, and empathetic. Unfortunately, she wasn't able to give me an update on the status of my computer. She told me that my only option was to wait three days and call again.

"They won't let me escalate it until it's been six business days. I tried to

escalate it sooner once before, and *they* told me it was too early."

Sherry didn't offer any alternatives, so I suggested a couple of my own. I asked if they could take the needed part from another computer, or perhaps just send me a new computer since they couldn't tell me when they'd be able to repair mine. The answer to both of my suggestions was "No." Sherry told me she'd tried those already; her response was, "*They* told me they aren't able to do it."

I was disappointed and frustrated, but I suspect Sherry was too. After all, she didn't manufacture my laptop improperly, she didn't cause the parts shortage, she wasn't responsible for the lack of information on the backordered part, and she clearly didn't write the policy that made customers wait six business days before escalating the inquiry to someone with greater authority and resources.

Many people get into customer service because they like to help others, but Sherry wasn't being given the opportunity to provide that help. Instead, she was tasked with sharing bad news without being able to offer any solutions. I could tell from the tone in her voice that she'd probably taken a lot of calls like mine.

This chapter explores the critical link between a company's service delivery systems and its employees' motivation. We'll learn how employees can be put in an impossible position when those systems are broken. Eventually, employees tend to stop trying, and they might even begin to work against your company's best interests. When customer service leaders don't discover or fix problems that are hindering employee performance, those problems can continue unchecked.

Broken Systems Demotivate Employees

Customer service researcher John Goodman estimates as much as 60 percent of customer dissatisfaction is a result of poor products, services, or processes.[62]

Unfortunately for customer service employees, they're usually the ones who bear the brunt of the customer's anger. Rationally, this is part of their job. Emotionally, it's difficult to repeatedly take the blame for something that's completely out of your control.

Examples abound. An airline might cancel a flight due to an aircraft maintenance issue, but it's the gate agent who has to handle the furious travelers who are now stranded. The cable company may do a poor job of managing work schedules, but it's the repair technician who has to face the fuming customer when they arrive an hour later than expected. A customer waiting in unbelievably long lines at the Department of Motor Vehicles is likely to be somewhat agitated by the time they reach the employee behind the counter.

A 2015 study by the behavioral analytics company Mattersight discovered that 69 percent of customers who call customer service are frustrated before they even start talking to an employee.[63] Whatever issue prompted them to call is frequently compounded by an annoying voice menu system. The customer may have found themselves repeatedly yelling "Human!" into the phone in an attempt to reach a live person. Then, after waiting what seems like an eternity, they're finally connected to an employee who must bear the brunt of their frustration.

Customer service representatives are often part of a much larger system that serves a company's customers. This system is made up of people in various departments, the company's policies and procedures, and the leaders who design and manage them all. When these systems are broken, frontline employees generally lack the resources or authority to resolve the issues that lead to poor service. In many cases, these employees are just as frustrated as their customers, because they must repeatedly listen to complaints while being powerless to help.

Sherry, the customer service rep at the computer manufacturer, sounded like she was caught in a broken system when she explained to me her company's far-flung operations. The backordered part needed to fix my computer was being shipped from a supplier in Asia. The facility that would complete the repair once the part finally arrived was located in Memphis. Sherry worked at the company's call center in Atlanta. As much as she wanted to help me, any action she suggested would have to be reviewed, approved, and executed by someone else in a different department and a different city. Repairing and returning my computer was physically out of her control.

Situations like these are made worse when customers make no distinction between the employee and the company. A customer who says "You screwed up my order" or "You can't do anything right" may be referring to the company, but the language and tone feel like a personal attack to the employee. Employees soon find themselves in a no-win situation where they can't fix the problem, yet they feel like they're receiving all the blame.

A 2013 study by the contact center research firm Benchmark Portal found that the percentage of contact center agents who were extremely satisfied in their jobs dropped by 30 percent after just three months on the job.[64] Three months happens to be roughly the length of time it takes the average contact center agent to fully get up to speed in their role. This accounts for new hire training and a practice called "nesting," where a new agent works closely with an experienced agent or coach to continue refining their skills after the formal training program has ended.

I saw this problem firsthand when I worked as a call center training supervisor for a company that sold clothing through a catalog. Employees would feel motivated to do a great job as they graduated from new hire training, only to become disenchanted once they encountered the company's multiple broken systems.

One of those broken systems was handling returned merchandise. The returns department was so chronically behind that packages sent back by customers would sit for up to four weeks in a truck trailer behind the warehouse before employees even opened the package and recorded the return in the customer database.

This created an information void that caused big problems for customer service reps. Reps had to rely on the database when customers called to inquire about the status of their return, but the rep couldn't give an answer if the returned merchandise hadn't been recorded yet. Customers were understandably upset when they were told that the company had no idea whether a return they'd mailed three weeks ago had arrived. (This happened during a time when most packages sent through the post office could not be tracked.)

The company also had some unfriendly return policies that made customers even angrier. A customer returning an item they didn't want couldn't receive a refund until the return had been recorded. Customers who wanted to exchange an item would have to be charged for the new item if they didn't want to wait the three to four weeks for their exchange to be processed. These inflexible policies made it even more difficult for customer service reps to provide a solution.

My department was asked to train call center representatives to handle these situations as best as they could, but implementing a few communication techniques was no substitute for fixing the real problem. I don't know of any secret phrase that can make a customer feel better when your business is unable to find a package mailed three weeks earlier and then is unwilling to help the customer until after it had finally processed the return. Needless to say, our training was of little help.

Our customer service reps were incredibly frustrated by their inability to provide any real assistance to these customers. Eventually, either they learned to stop caring or they left the job. The employees who remained became less and less empathetic to their customers as they grew tired of repeatedly handling the same complaints. Many of the employees who didn't quit were fired for poor performance.

The vice president of customer service finally tried to address the problem by instituting a process improvement initiative called "One Call Resolution." The goal was to resolve customer complaints on the very first call so customers wouldn't call us over and over about the same problem. But the entire initiative consisted of a banner hung in a conference room and a short meeting to explain the concept to our call center supervisors. Nothing was done to address the huge backlog of unprocessed returns and the inflexible policies, which remained unchanged.

In Jim Collins' landmark book *Good to Great*, the bestselling author and researcher examined why some companies make the leap to greatness while others don't. One of his findings was that great companies have leaders who are constantly on the lookout for systemic problems.[65] Conversely, companies that wallow in mediocrity or eventually fail often do so due to an inability or unwillingness to identify and confront these challenges.

Organizations that consistently identify and fix service delivery problems go way beyond hanging a banner or holding a pep rally. They monitor service levels, conduct a root cause analysis to find the source of problems, and rapidly implement real solutions. Employees at all levels—from the frontlines to top executives—are focused on continuously improving customer service.

The internet retailer Amazon is famous for a relentless focus on quality. One terrific example comes from its distribution centers. Customer packages pass through what's called a SLAM machine, which is short for Scan, Label, Apply, and Manifest. The machine scans each shipment, generates a shipping label, and applies it to the package. One of the machine's functions is to weigh each package and compare it to what the package *should* weigh, given the package's expected contents. When there's a discrepancy, the SLAM machine sends the package down a separate line where employees can investigate the problem.

I saw an example of employees solving a quality problem while visiting an Amazon distribution center. Operators detected an issue with the SLAM machine where labels were being misapplied. Employees quickly shut down the line and rerouted packages through another line while they addressed the problem. Working as a team, they identified the root cause, solved the issue, and even tested the solution before restarting the line. All of this happened within just a few minutes, but it prevented dozens of shipping errors.[66]

Think about the impact this quality process had on customer service. Dozens of errors were prevented, which meant dozens of customers unknowingly avoided the hassle of having to contact customer service. That, in turn, spared Amazon's customer service representatives from having to handle contacts from customers who were upset about lost, delayed, or incorrect shipments.

Learned Helplessness Arises from Chronically Broken Systems

The longer systemic service failures are allowed to continue, the more likely employees are to become frustrated and dissatisfied with their jobs. Employees in this situation may soon find themselves thinking, "They don't pay me enough to deal with this every day."

Broken systems can eventually lead employees to experience a condition that psychologists call "learned helplessness." It occurs when people believe they're powerless to stop something negative from happening, so they begin to act as if it were a foregone conclusion.[67] Employees suffering from learned helplessness stop trying to resolve problems or provide outstanding service, because they believe there's nothing they can do to make the customer happy.

Sherry, the computer manufacturer's customer service rep, is a good example of an employee experiencing learned helplessness. She explained all the reasons why she was unable to help me get my computer repaired and returned any quicker. Her attitude was that there was nothing to be done but wait. Any suggestion I made was quickly countered with, "I've tried that before, and it won't work."

Employees experiencing learned helplessness also tend to become focused on placing blame for their dissatisfaction rather than trying to resolve it. They blame management for not fixing the broken system or process. They blame other departments for not doing their jobs correctly. Some may even blame their customers for not being more understanding.

I once stepped into an airport newsstand to buy a magazine. While I was searching for one that looked interesting, I overheard the newsstand's two employees trying to outdo each other with stories of poor customer behavior. Their stories all started with some version of, "What I hate about customers is..." It became obvious that I would likely become more fodder for them no matter how well I behaved, so I left the store without making a purchase.

You'd expect employees to leave their jobs if they disliked them so much, but people experiencing learned helplessness may not realize this is an option. I returned to the same airport newsstand three months later and encountered the same two employees having the same conversation about customers they hate! This time, I was determined to have something to read for my flight, so I quickly selected a magazine and brought it to the register. The two employees looked at me disdainfully while one of them rang up my purchase. I waited patiently for her to tell me the total, but she instead pointed at the display on her register without saying a word. I paid the amount indicated, and as I left the store, I overheard the employees complaining about customers who are too dumb to see the amount displayed on the register.

When employees feel that customer dissatisfaction is a foregone conclusion, it becomes a self-reinforcing concept. Because these employees have stopped trying to fix problems they don't think can be solved, customers continue to get irritated with both the problem and the employee. The customer's unhappiness further reinforces the employee's belief that dissatisfaction is inevitable.

A customer service representative I'll call Janet (not her real name) complained to me that her customers were lazy. She took call after call each day from customers trying to track down their order, but these customers weren't prepared with basic information such as their account number, order number, or even the date when the order was placed. Janet found herself becoming increasingly impatient with her customers and treating them brusquely.

The real cause of Janet's frustration wasn't the customers; it was the reason why so many were calling. The company clearly had a broken system where orders weren't being delivered as quickly as customers expected, and there was no system to proactively alert customers to delays. So customers naturally started wondering where their order was and called Janet.

The best way to help employees avoid experiencing learned helplessness is to relentlessly focus on quality so employees won't have to deal with chronic problems. Pal's Sudden Service, a fast food restaurant chain located primarily in Tennessee, provides an excellent example. Look at the company's drive-thru order accuracy compared to several well-known competitors:[68]

- 99.9% Pal's Sudden Service
- 93.9% McDonald's
- 93.4% Chick-fil-A
- 89.7% Wendy's
- 89.5% Burger King
- 83.2% KFC

Fewer errors means fewer upset customers, which makes it easier for employees to focus on making customers happy rather than fixing chronic problems.

One of the company's secrets is an unusual process where essential skills are constantly monitored and trained. During each shift, employees are randomly selected for "recertification," where they must correctly demonstrate essential job skills. Employees who score less than 100 percent must be retrained. The company's CEO, Thomas Crosby, described the process as a way of avoiding bad habits, "It's our belief that human beings, just like machines, need to be recalibrated."[69]

Another way to avoid learned helplessness is to make employees feel like a valuable part of your organization's efforts to continuously improve customer service. Ask for their feedback. Involve them in process improvement initiatives. Give them the skills and authority to take greater control of the service they provide.

I once worked with a client's payroll department to help them overcome learned helplessness by involving them in improving their processes. The department had been under scrutiny for extensive errors and frequently missing or delayed paychecks. Department employees had become so busy trying to keep up with their workload that they were convinced the only solution was to add additional employees. However, there was no room in the budget to bring on more staff, so the team began to accept the errors and delays as inevitable.

Our first step together was coming to an agreement on the role of the department. The payroll team had looked at themselves as a data processing center where time cards went in and paychecks came out. This task-oriented approach made it hard for them to distinguish between essential and non-essential tasks or appreciate how frustrating it was for an employee to not get paid or be paid less than they were owed. The payroll team needed to view employees as internal customers, so we redefined the team's role to focus on ensuring all employees were paid accurately and on time.

The second step was to create a map of the current payroll process. The team instinctively knew that some of their work was inefficient, but this map helped them visualize some glaring problems. They were able to identify many duplicate steps that could be eliminated. Reflecting on their vision of paying all employees accurately and on time also helped the team reprioritize work so that nonessential tasks were put aside during busy times. Finally, the team implemented several safeguards against errors so fewer employees would be paid incorrectly and the payroll team would spend less time fixing mistakes.

The final step was to implement the new procedures and measure progress. The entire team was eager to try out the new process they'd created and felt much better about their ability to achieve great results. Their efforts and positive attitude resulted in a 25 percent reduction in payroll processing time, a sharp reduction in errors, and a savings of thousands of dollars. The department gradually began earning back the trust of internal customers. Best of all, the team now realized they could control their own destiny and weren't dependent on adding additional employees to be successful.

An employee may not always be able to fix a broken system, but they still may have the ability to influence a better outcome for their customer. A contact center representative may not be able to get returns processed any faster, but they may be allowed to send out a replacement order before the returned merchandise is received. An employee at an airport newsstand may not be able to control the long security lines that aggravate travelers, but they can try to brighten another person's day with an infectious smile and fast, friendly service.

The Dangers of Employee Disengagement

Employee engagement is defined as the extent to which an employee purposefully contributes to their organization's success. According to Gallup's 2017 State of the American Workplace Report, 67 percent of U.S. employees are disengaged. Of that group, 16 percent are described as "actively disengaged," which means they "are miserable in the workplace and destroy what the most engaged employees build."[70]

There are many reasons an employee becomes disengaged. They may have been hired to do a job they don't enjoy. The employee might have a poor relationship with their boss. One of the biggest contributors to employee disengagement is a failure to detect and fix processes that produce customer dissatisfaction.

Chronic customer service failure can trip several levers that contribute to employee disengagement. The employee can feel as though their contributions don't count, since they don't have the ability to improve the broken process. They might feel their voice isn't heard if their manager doesn't listen to or act on feedback about chronically broken systems. They can easily feel discouraged after repeatedly being on the receiving end of customer complaints they come to believe they aren't able to resolve.

You can imagine how unlikely it is to get even passable customer service from someone who's disengaged from their work and their employer. They simply don't care about serving customers and give the minimal amount of effort just to get by. Some of these employees intentionally deliver poor service as a means of lashing out at their employer and customers.

Comcast made national headlines in early 2015 when a customer, Ricardo Brown, noticed something unusual on his bill. His first name had been changed to "Asshole" by a Comcast agent, so the customer's name on the bill now read "Asshole Brown." This came shortly after Brown's wife, Lisa, had called to cancel the cable portion of the couple's Comcast service and was badgered by a "Retention Specialist" whose job was to talk the Browns out of cancelling.[71]

This may be an extreme example, but there are many other instances where disengaged employees deliberately provide poor service. A retail associate may avoid customers who are obviously in search of help. A restaurant server might keep customers waiting while carrying on a conversation with a coworker. A city worker could intentionally delay processing paperwork needed for a building permit.

Employee disengagement can also make it more costly for companies to deliver customer service. Gallup estimates that disengaged employees in the United States alone cost companies as much as $605 billion annually in lost productivity.[72]

When I worked as a training supervisor for the catalog company with the returns problem, chronic absenteeism and high turnover rates were two costs related to employee disengagement that directly affected the bottom line. On any given day, nearly 20 percent of the company's call center employees would call in sick. The company had to hire extra employees and pay expensive overtime to cover shifts for the absentees. Supervisors spent a lot of their time disciplining employees for absenteeism, which in turn created additional resentment.

The cost of excessive turnover was also substantial. The company's annual turnover rate among call center employees was well over 100 percent. Most employees quit or were fired before they had been there even one full year, and many didn't even make it 90 days. This created a constant need to hire and train new employees, which significantly elevated recruiting and training costs. Further, the high turnover rate gave the company a reputation in the community as an undesirable place to work, so it soon became much harder to find talented—and engaged—employees.

At the opposite end of the spectrum are engaged employees. Engaged customer service employees understand and agree with their company's goals, strategies, and attitudes towards customer service. These employees consistently try to align their performance with the needs of their employer.

Employers need two essential elements to engage their customer service employees. First, customer service leaders must share their customer service goals with employees and provide feedback on progress toward those goals. Second, employees must be enlisted as partners in achieving goals rather than being treated as pawns moved at management's whim.

Enterprise Rent-a-Car is an organization that has leveraged employee engagement to earn a reputation for outstanding customer service. At the end of 2017, J.D. Power recognized the company as the leader in customer satisfaction among rental car companies for the fourth year in a row.[73] At the heart of its engagement efforts is the Enterprise Service Quality Index (ESQi), which is a system used to evaluate customer satisfaction. Enterprise customers are regularly surveyed on their rental experience, and the results are captured and reported at the local branch level.[74]

The ESQi results are reported throughout the company. Employees are trained on the factors that drive customer satisfaction and are encouraged to use their discretion to fix problems on the spot. A relentless desire to improve service has even spurred innovative ideas from front-line employees, such as Enterprise's famous service where they pick you up at your home or office.[75]

Leaders Blind to Reality

By now, you may be wondering why more companies don't fix the broken systems that hurt customer service and crush employee engagement.

This is precisely the area where leaders in many organizations fall short. Some rely too much on reports and data, rather than listening to employees and customers. Others just assume that employees will perform better if they're given more incentives or face stiffer sanctions. Like employees, some leaders simply don't care.

Dave was an account manager whose job was to take orders, provide customer service, and find ways to increase sales with each of his customers. He was a good example of what can happen to customer service employees when their managers are blind to the root causes of poor service.

Business hadn't been very good recently for Dave and his coworkers. Sales were down, customer complaints were up, and customers were taking their business to competitors. Like many of his coworkers, Dave began to exhibit signs of learned helplessness and disengagement. He spent a good part of his day commiserating with coworkers about slumping sales, taking extra-long breaks, and finding ways to avoid work altogether.

Dave's manager knew he needed to turn things around. When he looked at the department's sales reports to find the answer, it seemed to jump out almost immediately. The company's phone call tracking software revealed that Dave and most of his coworkers were making far fewer phone calls than they had been just three months ago, when the sales figures were much better. The manager knew that taking care of customers required frequent contact, so the solution seemed obvious. The account managers needed to make more calls!

The next Monday, the manager announced a special incentive program. Any account manager who made 125 phone calls by the end of the week would earn a $100 cash bonus.

The plan worked wonderfully. All the account managers made at least 125 calls and earned the $100 bonus. Dave, whose calls had gone down significantly in recent months, reached 125 calls by Thursday! The manager patted himself on the back as employee after employee complimented him on a great incentive program.

The only problem was that sales didn't go up during that week. In fact, sales actually went *down* from the week before. Dave's manager was convinced the incentive program was a great plan, so he couldn't understand what had happened.

Dave knew why (and, after reading the passage in Chapter 4 about the problem with financial incentives, you may have guessed why, too). Dave earned the $100 bonus, but not by calling customers. Instead, he called friends, family members, and even dialed his own number a few times to make sure the call tracking software recorded 125 phone calls.

Dave didn't call many customers, because he knew there was nothing to talk about. His customers had been upset for the past year about long lead times and quality issues. The last straw had come three months ago, when the company significantly raised its prices. Now the products Dave was supposed to sell were more expensive, took longer to ship, and had more errors per order than those sold by his competitors.

Dave began exhibiting signs of disengagement and learned helplessness as more and more customers defected and sales declined. He made fewer phone calls, because he was tired of fielding complaints about high prices and poor quality. Dave had gone to his manager for help, but the manager didn't seem to listen. In a typical disengagement pattern, Dave began spending most of his day complaining to coworkers while waiting for things to somehow get better.

The manager never questioned why a successful and experienced account manager like Dave suddenly stopped making calls. It never occurred to the manager that the increase in prices had taken away Dave's last remaining competitive advantage. Now the company's customers were leaving in droves to buy better quality products that were delivered faster for less money.

Managers who remain blind to the big picture aren't likely to solve the systemic problems that drive customers away. Too often, leaders fail to dig deeper when they encounter the symptoms of poor service. They try simple fixes—such as offering incentives—which only create more problems. What these leaders don't do often enough is carefully examine the real root cause of the problem before creating a solution.

Successful customer service leaders approach problems by first asking questions. They resist the urge to assign blame, jump to conclusions, or dismiss the problem altogether; instead, they try to understand what's really going on. This doesn't have to be a lengthy process; they are just careful to face reality before designing and implementing solutions.

One of my favorite exercises to use in this situation is to imagine an iceberg. Only the tip of an iceberg is visible above the surface of the water, but what lies unseen is often bigger and more dangerous. Uncovering icebergs usually involves asking a few questions when confronted with a service problem:

- Is it possible this same problem has happened before?
- How likely is it that this problem will happen again?
- Can similar problems exist in other places?
- Who else might be affected by this problem?
- What can I learn from this problem that can be applied to other issues?

I remember conducting an iceberg investigation when I was the Customer Service Manager for a catalog company plagued by backorders on a popular product. My customer service reps were besieged with calls from angry customers, and it was taking a toll on their morale. It was tempting to write off the backorders as a simple matter of demand exceeding supply, but this did little to help my employees provide better service.

The questions in the iceberg framework took me to many places within the company, from merchandising, to information technology, to our warehouse and order fulfillment operations. Working closely with managers from these departments, we discovered a host of problems. These problems had far wider implications than a single product, illuminating multiple opportunities for improvement that might never have been discovered without looking for icebergs.

We implemented a system where we proactively communicated updates to our customers on backordered products via phone calls, emails, and postcards, which greatly reduced customer inquiries. Our information technology team discovered and repaired a computer glitch that miscalculated inventory levels and made it appear that an item was in stock when it wasn't. The order fulfillment team improved its inventory tracking procedures and discovered large quantities of backordered products lost in the warehouse.

Customer satisfaction is clearly linked to a company's ability to deal with operational problems head-on. In *Good to Great*, Jim Collins aptly describes this as a willingness to "confront the brutal facts."[76] The process may be painful, but the long-term payoff is customer service delivery systems that work.

Solution Summary:
How to Avoid Mutually Assured Dissatisfaction

The best customer service organizations make it incredibly easy for employees to provide outstanding service. Here's a summary of the solutions presented in this chapter:

- Take action to identify and address operational issues that contribute to customer service failures and frustrate employees.
- Include frontline employees in your organization's efforts to continuously improve customer service.
- Engage employees by sharing customer service goals and enlisting employees' help in achieving them.
- Avoid becoming blind to reality by avidly searching for icebergs—the small signs that could be indicators of big problems.
- Approach operational problems by asking questions and gaining a true understanding of what's going on before jumping to conclusions about the solution.

CHAPTER 6 NOTES

62   John Goodman. *Strategic Customer Service.* AMACOM, 2009.

63   "Please hold for a reality check: the real reasons consumers are fed up with call centers." Mattersight Corporation, 2015.

64   "Agent Voices: Contact Center Agent Satisfaction Research Report." Benchmark Portal, 2013.

65   Jim Collins. *Good to Great. Why some companies make the leap and others don't.* arperBusiness, New York, 2001.

66   Jeff Toister. "An Inside Look at Amazon's Fulfillment Center Operations." *Inside Customer Service* blog. April 18, 2017.

67   Guy Winch. *The Squeaky Wheel. Complaining the right way to get results, improve your relationships, and enhance self-esteem.* Walker and Company, New York, 2011.

68   Sam Oches. "2017 Drive-Thru Performance Study." *QSR Magazine.* October 2017.

69   Leigh Buchannen. "Training the Best Damn Fry Cooks (and Future Leaders) in the U.S." *Inc. Magazine.* April 23, 2014.

70   "State of the American Workplace." Gallup. 2017.

71   Ashley Feinberg. "Comcast Changed Customer's Name to 'Asshole Brown' But Is Totally Sorry." *Gizmodo.* January 28, 2015.

72   "State of the American Workplace." Gallup. 2017.

73 "Rental Car Satisfaction Improves Amid Increased Price Pressure, J.D. Power Finds."
J.D. Power press release. November 8, 2017.

74 An overview of ESQi can be found on the Enterprise Rent-a-Car website.
http://aboutus.enterprise.com/customer_service.html.

75 Fred Reichheld. *The Ultimate Question 2.0.* Harvard Business School Publishing,
Boston, 2011.

76 Jim Collins. *Good to Great. Why some companies make the leap and others don't.*
HarperBusiness, New York, 2001.

CHAPTER 7

Attention Is in Short Supply

* * *

Getting Employees to Notice What Customers Really Need

My wife, Sally, and I flew into San Francisco for a getaway weekend and arrived at our hotel before check-in time. Hotels will often let you check in early if the room is ready, but the front desk agent informed us that our room wouldn't be available for another 45 minutes. We told her we'd relax in the lobby, and she assured us she'd let us know as soon as our room was ready. There were some overstuffed chairs directly in front of the check-in counter that looked comfortable, so we grabbed a seat and settled in for the wait.

I'm fascinated by observing people provide customer service, so I passed the time by watching the front desk agent and her coworkers. They seemed engaged in a never-ending flurry of activity. A steady stream of people approached the counter to check in or out, ask for directions, or make some other request. The phones rang frequently, and our front desk agent had to pause to answer. She also seemed to have quite a bit of computer work to do, since she filled the time between guests and phone calls by working away at the keyboard in front of her.

Sally and I started to get a little anxious as we neared the 45-minute mark, since it was a beautiful day and we were eager to go explore the city. We started watching the front desk agent in anticipation that, any minute now, she'd wave us over and let us know our room was ready. She was such a whirlwind of activity that we assumed she was on top of it.

But 45 minutes soon became an hour, with no sign from the hotel associate. We finally went back to the counter and asked for an update. She took a moment to look us up on her computer and said, "You can check in now, your room has been ready for half an hour."

She had forgotten us! We were literally sitting in front of her for an hour, and she had forgotten we were there. Even worse, we could have checked in 30 minutes earlier. She didn't even apologize.

Situations like this occur every day in customer service. From a customer's perspective, it couldn't be more obvious. The employee simply needs to pay more attention.

In this chapter, we'll see that one of the challenges to providing outstanding customer service is that our attention is in increasingly short supply. In some cases, employees' attention is divided between too many tasks, which can cause them to miss opportunities to serve. At other times, employees can become so focused on one thing that they develop tunnel vision and miss important cues from their customers. We'll even discover a way that our brains can naturally cause us to stop listening by jumping to conclusions.

None of these obstacles are insurmountable, but companies need to provide customer service representatives with a lot of training and assistance to help them pay careful attention to their customers' needs.

The Curse of Multitasking

As I write this chapter, there are more than 17,000 customer service jobs advertised on the website Indeed.com listing "multitasking" in the job description.

Multitasking, the way most people define it, isn't possible, because our brains are only capable of handling one conscious thought at a time. According to studies conducted by David Meyer, a researcher at the University of Michigan's Brain, Cognition, and Action Laboratory, when we attempt to multitask, our brain is actually rapidly switching between the various tasks we're trying to attend to. A little bit of time is lost whenever we move from one task to the next, because our brains must refocus.[77]

The only situation where we can effectively perform more than one task at a time is when just one of those tasks requires conscious attention. That's why we're able to carry on a conversation with someone over the phone while we doodle on a notepad, but we aren't very good at having that same conversation while trying to send someone else an email.

I discovered a great demonstration, courtesy of Dave Crenshaw, illustrating the challenges of multitasking. The activity involves timing how long it takes you to write down the sentence, "Multitasking is worse than a lie" on one line and the numbers 1–27 in order on a second line. Most people naturally write down the full sentence and then proceed to write down the numbers.

In round two, you write down the same sentence and the numbers beneath it, but this time you switch back and forth between writing a letter on the first line and writing a number below it. So you'd write "M" on line one, then "1" on line two before going back to line one to write "u" next to the "M" and so on. The second round always takes significantly longer. You can try this exercise yourself by visiting Crenshaw's website: https://davecrenshaw.com/multitasking-example.

In a service environment, our inability to multitask means employees must either choose between two conscious tasks or do both with far less efficiency. Think back to a time when you were served by someone who was speaking to another customer on the phone. One of two things probably happened. The first possibility was that the customer service rep either asked you to wait, or put the caller on hold so they could serve one person at a time. The second possibility was that they tried to serve you while speaking to the other person, which resulted in their paying substantially less attention to you.

Our inability to effectively focus on two things at once isn't the only challenge faced by employees when it comes to multitasking. Today's modern work environment is full of auditory and visual stimuli that constantly compete for our attention. The way our brains interact with these attention-catching stimuli naturally encourages people to switch rapidly between tasks.

Attention is captured in two primary ways. The first is known as "top-down" attention, where we consciously focus on a particular goal or task. The second is known as "bottom-up" attention, where an external stimulus grabs our attention, such as a phone ringing or a person suddenly standing in front of us.[78]

Our top-down attention can override our bottom-up attention, allowing us to tune out external distractions, but this requires deliberate concentration. However, the more our attention is captured by external bottom-up stimuli, the harder it is for our brain to consciously refocus its attention on a specific goal. The inevitable result of too many distractions is that we find it hard to concentrate and complete a single task that we might be able to quickly accomplish if there weren't so many other things competing for our attention.[79]

Now let's think back to the hotel's front desk associate. She was bombarded by external stimuli. The phones were ringing, coworkers interrupted her, and guests continuously approached her. The conflict between her top-down goal of completing certain responsibilities (e.g., letting us know when our room was ready) and the bottom-up attention grabbers (e.g., someone interrupting her to ask a question) caused her to constantly switch tasks. Each time this happened, my wife and I were pushed farther and farther away from her conscious mind, until we eventually disappeared completely.

Many customer service employees are continuously interrupted by external stimuli that naturally encourage them to multitask. A server in a busy restaurant must keep tabs on multiple tables while constantly being interrupted by guests. A retail cashier must try to ring up customer transactions while other customers interrupt to ask questions. Even someone working in an office environment is subjected to frequent interruptions by coworkers, new messages flashing onto their computer screen, and even that catchy song on the radio.

Some people argue that multitasking really refers to the ability to manage multiple priorities. By definition, a priority is something that merits attention ahead of competing alternatives.[80] This concept often invites confusion and poor performance when customer service priorities are not clearly identified and an employee is therefore unable to consciously choose between tasks based on their level of importance.

Here's an example you almost certainly have experienced. Think back to a time when you were placing an order at a fast food restaurant or coffee shop, and another customer walked up to the counter and interrupted your order to ask the cashier for something. This represents a customer service dilemma that's based on attention and which customer has priority.

The other customer's interruption is an external attention grabber that the cashier is certain to notice. The employee must now choose between continuing to take your order or serving the interrupting customer. They can't do both, so one task must become more important than the other.

Their choice depends on their priorities. The cashier will continue serving you if their priority is finishing with the customer they're already working with. However, they might stop taking your order and help the other customer if they spilled a drink on the floor and the priority switches to mopping up the spilled drink to prevent an accident.

What will happen if the priorities aren't clearly defined? The cashier will help the other customer, even if the other customer's need is a non-emergency (such as a request for extra ketchup). Without a specific intention to consciously focus on one task over another, the interrupting customer will capture the employee's attention, and the employee's natural inclination will be to help that person.

With all the interruptions in the workplace, our natural instinct to focus on external stimuli, and a lack of clear priorities, it's no wonder that customer service representatives find it difficult to be fully engaged with the task at hand. Their attention is constantly being pulled in any number of directions, which causes them to work less efficiently, make more errors, and ultimately provide their customers with poor treatment. Companies must help their employees do a better job of focusing their attention on appropriate priorities if they want to deliver outstanding service.

The best way to help employees pay the right amount of attention to the right thing at the right time is to make it easier for them to work within their natural abilities. This means creating a work environment where employees are able to focus on priorities and ignore distractions.

The first step employers should take is to discourage employees from performing more than one conscious task at a time. One company I worked with tried to maximize efficiency by having its customer service agents respond to customer emails in between phone calls. In an experiment, my client tried having agents focus solely on either handling phone calls or responding to emails.

The experiment immediately yielded an increase in both quality and productivity. Phone agents were now able to focus better on customers who called, where they previously had to mentally disengage from the email they were writing and refocus their attention on an incoming call. Email agents were able to understand customer needs better and write more thorough responses that were less likely to generate additional emails from the customer. Productivity also increased, and my client was able to respond to emails much faster than before!

Best of all, my client retained the flexibility to meet changing customer demand throughout the day. If phone volume suddenly spiked, my client could ask a few email agents to stop writing emails and answer phone calls until customers were no longer waiting on hold.

Another way companies can help employees pay attention to the right thing is through the use of automatic reminders, which are automated auditory or visual reminders that capture attention with a helpful external attention grabber at just the right time. The alarm on your calendar or cell phone reminds you to head to a meeting. The baristas at coffee shops use little timers to remind them to check on the brewing coffee. Contact center representatives often have little windows that pop up on their computer screen to remind them to make a special offer or provide their customers with certain information.

Why automatic? Automatic reminders are simply more reliable than our own memories or even other people. When we think back to the front desk associate who forgot to tell us our room was ready, it's very possible she thought she'd remember to check on us without realizing she'd soon be consumed with other work. Or she might have relied on a phone call from someone in housekeeping to let her know the room was ready, but that system would fail if the housekeeper forgot to call. Relying on your frazzled memory—or on other, equally harried people to remind you to do something—is a recipe for forgetfulness.

A third way for companies to help their employees is to firmly establish customer service priorities. If you recall, employees can have a difficult time paying attention to the right tasks when they face confusing or competing options. Clear priorities that are trained, communicated frequently, and followed consistently can help employees make the right choices in situations where there are competing tasks.

The Walt Disney Company sets clear priorities for its cast members (Disney's term for employees) so they know what's important in any given situation. I once saw this in action while riding the Twilight Zone Tower of Terror, a thrill ride that simulates being stuck in a runaway elevator inside a haunted hotel. Everyone had just belted into their seats when a young boy started crying and protesting that he didn't want to go on the scary ride. The cast member playing the "demented elevator operator" immediately broke out of his character and invited the boy to step off the ride. He assured the boy's concerned mother that he'd keep a close eye on her son while she enjoyed the ride. When we returned and the elevator doors opened, the cast member was waiting with the now-smiling boy standing next to him.

Disney's priorities clearly guided the cast member's actions. Safety is the first priority, and this was evident when he delayed the ride and made sure the boy exited safely. The second priority is courtesy, so the cast member momentarily paused his scripted routine to politely address the young boy and assure the mother her son would be safe. The show is Disney's third priority, so the cast member quickly resumed his act once the first two priorities were addressed.[81]

Paying TOO Much Attention Isn't a Good Idea, Either

Customer service representatives are often guilty of not paying enough attention, but paying too much attention to a single customer or task can have consequences, too. Here's an example.

I was dining at one of my favorite local restaurants with my wife and her parents. We received lousy service throughout our meal and hardly saw our server after she took our orders. Our water glasses sat empty and we finished our food before she came back to take our drink order. It even took a long time just to get our check.

Why was our service so poor? The most likely explanation was that our server was paying too much attention to a large group seated in the middle of her section. They arrived in a steady stream rather than all at once, so she was constantly going back to them to take a new drink or food order. Large groups can be difficult for servers to handle, and we could clearly see her focusing her attention on making sure these people were happy.

Paying so much attention to the large group caused her to develop tunnel vision, making it hard for her to see us or remember our needs. She repeatedly walked within eyesight of our table on her way to the kitchen without even glancing in our direction. We even resorted to waving at her in an attempt to capture her attention, but she seemed completely absorbed with taking care of this large party.

Our poor service may have been attributable to something called *inattentional blindness*. Think of it as the opposite of the front desk associate who was constantly distracted. It's possible to be so focused on a specific task that you tune out external stimuli that would otherwise be obvious.

An amazing experiment conducted by Christopher Chabris and Daniel Simons illustrates this effect. (You can try it yourself before reading further by watching this short video on YouTube: http://youtu.be/vJG698U2Mvo.)

In the experiment, subjects are asked to watch a short video that features two teams of three people. One team is wearing white t-shirts, while the other team is dressed in black t-shirts. Both teams are passing basketballs back and forth among their teammates while mingling with members of the other team. The subjects in the experiment were asked to watch the video and count the number of times the team in white passes the basketball.

About halfway through the video, a person dressed in a gorilla suit walks into view from the right side of the screen. The gorilla slowly walks through the two teams passing their basketballs, coming to a stop in the middle of the scene. It faces the camera and pounds its chest before turning to its right and slowly walking off screen.

Amazingly, Chabris and Simons discovered that nearly 50 percent of the test subjects failed to notice the person in the gorilla costume. The test subjects who missed the gorilla were so focused on counting the white team's basketball passes that they tuned everything else out, including the gorilla![82]

There are many situations where inattentional blindness, or "invisible gorillas," may lead to poor customer service. A grocery store cashier discussing the break schedule with their supervisor may miss a chance to greet the customer standing in front of them. A retail associate consumed with folding a stack of sweaters may not notice a customer who clearly needs help finding a pair of jeans. A customer service representative may get so focused on clearing out a slew of emails that they hardly bother to read each one before pasting in a stock reply and hitting "send."

The challenge of inattentional blindness can be compounded by a belief that an employee should have seen something so obvious. Without the benefit of Chabris and Simons's experiment, who would believe that so many people wouldn't notice a gorilla strolling through a short video? Likewise, customer service supervisors often chalk up episodes of inattentional blindness to an employee's carelessness. A restaurant manager might tell a server, "You need to pay more attention," without understanding the real reason why they repeatedly ignored several of their tables while attending to the needs of a large group.

Inattentional blindness could be another reason my wife and I became invisible to the hotel's front desk associate. There were several occasions when she wasn't being interrupted by a phone call, another guest, or a coworker. During those times, she turned her attention to her computer and intently focused on her stack of paperwork. The concentration required to complete those computer tasks may have caused her to deliberately tune out any additional stimuli, such as two guests patiently waiting in the lobby right in front of her.

There are a couple of ways to help employees avoid inattentional blindness. The first step is reducing the amount of tasks employees are expected to accomplish in addition to serving customers. Tasks tend to take employees' focus away from helping people, because supervisors can easily observe whether a task is completed, while customer interactions are usually harder to monitor.

The Home Depot used this strategy to dramatically improve their customer service levels. In 2007, its customer service ratings hit rock bottom with a 67 point satisfaction score on the American Customer Satisfaction Index. Just three years later, the company's score had risen dramatically to 75.[83]

A core component of Home Depot's turnaround was reducing the number of tasks assigned to their sales associates and putting more people on the floor so it was easier for customers to get assistance. This approach even extended to its store management teams, where over 200 weekly reports and emails were eliminated in favor of a simple one-page scorecard.[84]

Another way to avoid inattentional blindness is to create the expectation that employees proactively greet any customer that comes near them. In hospitality industries, where employees have face-to-face customer contact, this technique is referred to as the 10 & 5 Rule: associates are expected to give any guest within ten feet a nonverbal acknowledgement—such as a smile or a wave—and verbally greet any guest who's within five feet. In retail, there's a similar concept known as "zone coverage," where associates are expected to greet any customer who comes into their department or assigned part of the store. Employees can avoid inattentional blindness by continuously scanning for customers in need of assistance, rather than waiting for customers to approach them.

Listening to Customers Can Be Difficult

So far in this chapter, we've examined obstacles that make it hard for employees to focus on their customers. When a customer does manage to capture an employee's attention, it may still be difficult for the employee to truly listen. Our own brain can sometimes be the source of distractions that prevent us from understanding our customers' needs.

Time pressure is one example. When an employee feels rushed or hurried, they may find their mind wandering in anticipation of the next task. A long line can cause a cashier to work a little faster and pay a little less attention to each individual customer in an effort to keep the line moving. Contact centers often have large display boards that indicate the number of callers on hold along with the average wait time, which can encourage reps to hurry through calls when those numbers get beyond acceptable limits. Even employees who handle email correspondence can miss important pieces of their customers' messages when they're working too fast to clear a backlog of inquiries.

Yet another obstacle is that our brain can sometimes override our concentration by jumping to conclusions. I once experienced a classic example of this phenomenon when I called a customer service number to get some help accessing my online account. I was halfway through my question when the customer service representative interrupted me and said, "That's actually a separate password than the one I'm resetting for you. That one is just for billing."

Great, except that wasn't the question I was about to ask. "I know, but I was going to ask if I can reset the billing password myself so that I…"

He interrupted again, "But you don't need the billing password to access your online account." *Sigh.* Still not the question I was trying to ask.

Why do so many knowledgeable customer service representatives find it difficult to listen to their customers without interrupting? This problem is related to how we naturally process information.

The human brain has a design feature that allows us to take a small amount of information and compare it to familiar patterns. This capability allows us to make quick sense of large amounts of data without getting bogged down in the details. It's an ability that comes in handy in many ways, such as determining if something is safe or dangerous, recognizing people we know, or even reading.

Here's a simple example. Try reading the sentence below:

People can easliy raed misspleled wrods as long as all the lettres are there and the fisrt and lsat letters are in the corerct position.

Thanks to our handy pattern-recognition ability, you can read sentences like the one above. Your brain recognizes the pattern presented by the arrangement of the letters and the context of the sentence. It doesn't matter that the letters aren't perfectly placed; they're close enough for your brain to quickly understand the meaning.[85]

It's this same ability that can get customer service representatives into trouble when it comes to listening. The customer service representative I talked to about resetting my billing password had undoubtedly heard questions similar to mine many times. The start of my sentence fit a familiar pattern, so his brain stopped listening and presented an answer to the question he thought I was going to ask. The problem occurred because my question was a new variation on this familiar pattern, so the answer that leapt into his mind was incorrect.

Effective listening skills are often taken for granted; as a result, many employees are given little support or training in this area. Employees can overestimate their own abilities, because they often receive some of their customer's message and mistakenly believe they heard all of their customer's needs. Companies that want to deliver outstanding customer service must offer training and coaching to help their employees become better listeners.

Training customer service employees on active listening skills is a good place to start. Active listening requires someone to be fully engaged with the person they're listening to. This includes physically facing the speaker, making eye contact, and providing nonverbal cues that indicate attention such as nodding. Employees should learn to ask clarifying questions and paraphrase what their customer is saying to confirm understanding. Most important, employees must develop the ability to consciously suspend judgment until they're certain they understand what their customer is asking for. These skills allow customer service reps to focus on their customer, making it easier to tune out distractions and resist the urge to jump to conclusions.

Regular coaching and feedback will help customer service reps keep their listening skills sharp. Constructive feedback can illuminate the blind spots that we can all develop when it comes to focusing on our customers, such as a habit of trying to finish the other person's sentences. Supervisors should regularly observe customer interactions and help their employees identify opportunities for continual improvement.

Finally, reduce time pressure whenever possible by providing adequate staffing levels so employees can work efficiently without being pressured to compromise service quality. Tight budgets can make it tempting for customer service leaders to cut back on staffing, but this may result in increased customer complaints and, ultimately, reduced revenue as dissatisfied customers take their business elsewhere. In Chapter 11, we'll examine this issue in greater detail.

Solution Summary: Helping Employees Pay Better Attention

Customer service should be priority number one for customer service employees, but actions speak louder than words. Employees often need help to pay careful attention to each customer. Here's a summary of the solutions discussed in this chapter:

- Develop work processes and procedures that discourage employees from trying to complete more than one task at a time.
- Create automatic reminders that capture employees' attention at the right moment, such as a pop-up screen that reminds an employee to return a customer's call.
- Establish and reinforce clear customer service priorities so employees know where to focus their attention.
- Reduce the number of tasks customer service employees are expected to complete so they can devote more attention to serving customers.
- Help employees put customers first by maintaining an expectation that they proactively greet anyone who is in their vicinity.
- Train employees to use active listening skills when serving customers.
- Provide appropriate staffing levels so employees aren't tempted to compromise service quality in an effort to serve more people.

CHAPTER 7 NOTES

77   Meyer's website offers a very good introductory explanation, as well as several research papers. http://www.umich.edu/~bcalab/multitasking.html.

78   Steven L. Franconeri, Justin A. Junge, and Daniel J. Simons. "Searching for stimulus-driven shifts of attention." *Psychonomic Bulletin & Review.* 11 (5), pgs 876–881. 2004.

79   Valerio Santangelo, Marta Olivetti Belardinelli, Charles Spence, and Emiliano Macaluso. "Interactions between voluntary and stimulus-driven spatial attention mechanisms across sensory modalities." *Journal of Cognitive Neuroscience.* 21:12, pgs 2384–2397. 2008.

80   Merriam-Webster online dictionary: www.merriam-webster.com.

81   Ted Topping. "Day Two: Disney's Service Values." www.disney-dispatch.com.

82   Christopher Chabris and Daniel Simons. *The Invisible Gorilla and other ways our intuition deceives us.* Crown Publishers, New York. 2010.

83   The American Customer Satisfaction Index, Specialty Retail Stores. www.theacsi.org.

84   Patricia O'Connell. "Putting the Customer FIRST at Home Depot." *Bloomberg Businessweek.* November 5, 2010.

85   It's a great service to the world when people like Matt Davis take the time to summarize a heap of research in one coherent paper. You'll also learn that my misspelled sentence is not 100 percent accurate. http://www.mrc-cbu.cam.ac.uk/people/matt.davis/Cmabrigde/.

CHAPTER 8

What Role Will You Play Today?

• • •

Emphasizing the Primary Responsibility to Delight Customers

There was a long line of customers at the post office waiting for a clerk but only one customer at the self-service kiosk. I just needed to buy postage for a few items, so I got in line at the kiosk.

The elderly customer in front of me at the kiosk seemed overwhelmed. She was scanning through the various options on the screen and appeared to be uncomfortable using the machine. Fortunately for her, an employee stepped out of a back office and offered to assist.

The postal employee asked the customer questions and pushed the appropriate buttons on the machine. She helped the customer select the right options and even inserted her card for payment. The customer was soon finished with her transaction and looked visibly relieved.

Now it was my turn. I said hello to the employee and started my transaction. Without so much as asking if I needed assistance, the employee immediately interjected herself into my self-service transaction. She began asking me questions about what I was purchasing while pushing buttons on the kiosk in front of me.

I had used the machine many times and knew exactly what I was doing, so I politely thanked the employee and told her I didn't need any assistance.

Undaunted, the employee continued to try to serve me the same way she had the previous customer. She even assumed the same approach, treating me like a confused first-time user by trying to physically stand between me and the kiosk. The employee seemed oblivious to the fact that her interference was actually slowing down the transaction.

This time, I firmly told her I did not want her assistance and asked her to stop.

Her demeanor instantly changed. Her smile disappeared and she angrily walked away. What had started as a pleasant and helpful encounter quickly became a service failure.

It was a strange interaction. Why had the employee assumed I needed assistance without bothering to ask me first? Why did she continue to involve herself in what should have been a simple self-service transaction, even after I politely declined her help? And why was she unable to see that the service the first customer had so eagerly welcomed felt patronizing and unhelpful to me?

The answer likely comes down to what the employee imagined was her role in this situation: she was on a mission to expedite transactions. This employee wasn't a postal clerk, so she couldn't help out at the counter, but she could try to get people through the self-service line quickly. What she didn't recognize or understand was that I had very different needs than the first customer she helped.

In this chapter, we'll examine the strong connection between the level of customer service employees provide and their understanding of the role they're playing. We'll see how employees often define their role in terms of the tasks they're asked to complete rather than the assistance their customers want. We'll also learn how, in some extreme cases, otherwise good people can find themselves treating their customers horribly due to a misaligned sense of their responsibilities or blind obedience to an unethical or uncaring boss.

Companies that wish to deliver outstanding customer service must ensure their employees know their ultimate responsibility is serving the customer.

When Tasks Define Our Roles

Many customer service employees I speak with define their roles by the tasks they perform. If they're cashiers, they say, "I ring up purchases." If they're receptionists, they say, "I greet visitors." If they work in technical support, they say, "I fix computers."

But these descriptions don't describe *how* these employees should be helping their customers. Customers want cashiers to make paying for purchases a fast and hassle-free experience. Customers want receptionists to make them feel welcome and connect them with the person they came to visit. Customers want technical support reps to help minimize the lost productivity and aggravation that comes with a malfunctioning computer.

This task focus is often the cause of poor customer service, because the ultimate goal of delighting customers fades into the background. Let's say you order a new smartphone online, but when it arrives, you can't transfer the data from your old phone to your new one. You follow the directions on the support page of the company's website and still can't get it to work. So you finally give in and call technical support.

In that moment, you're feeling disappointed because you can't use your new phone, frustrated at your failed attempts to get it working, and annoyed that you have to go through the hassle of contacting technical support.

What's the technical support representative's role in this situation? The focus *should be* on turning around a disappointing, annoying, and frustrating experience to help restore the excitement you felt when your new phone first arrived. In fact, a 2017 study from the customer experience researcher, Temkin Group, found that *relief* is the number one emotion experienced by people who contact technical support.[86]

Unfortunately, a task-oriented employee is likely to think their primary goal is to tell you the solution so they can move on to the next call. The length of their call might be closely measured, giving them an extra incentive to get you off the phone quickly. This can cause them to miss the opportunity to empathize with your frustration, whole-heartedly apologize, or perhaps take a moment to walk you through a few of the new features of your phone that will help you get more out of it.

One technical support rep confided in me that she brusquely pushes customers through solutions in an effort to meet her own performance standards. "I have six minutes to complete each phone call," she said. "If a customer is really angry, I don't have time to try to make them feel better. All I can do is try to solve their problem and get them off the phone." The rep doesn't enjoy treating customers this way but feels she needs to if she wants her boss to think she's a good performer.

Customers in this situation may inadvertently contribute to the task orientation by telling the support rep, "I just want to get my phone working." That may be a statement spoken out of frustration, yet it can also become a signal to the customer service rep that telling the customer what to do is the most important task.

Sometimes, this task orientation can lead to reprehensible service. An estimated 6,000 people are mistakenly declared dead by the Social Security Administration each year. If you're one of them, this can be a financial nightmare, since your banking, credit cards, and credit reports are all tied to your Social Security number. As ridiculous as it may sound, the biggest hassle of all might be convincing a Social Security employee that you are still alive.

People victimized by this error describe getting the runaround, having to make multiple trips to their local Social Security office, and being required to complete mountains of paperwork just to prove they aren't deceased.[87] Instead of receiving compassion, a heartfelt apology, and a swift resolution, the victims are frequently stonewalled by bureaucrats who view their primary role as complying with processing procedures. Fixing this error can take as long as two months, and it's even been reported that more paperwork is required to reinstate someone erroneously considered deceased than is needed to accidentally declare them dead in the first place![88]

Sometimes task orientation can lead to downright strange behavior. I once went into my local sporting goods store to get a pair of insoles for my running shoes. A sales associate approached me after I'd been browsing for a few minutes and asked if I needed assistance. I told him what I was looking for and asked if the insoles I had in my hand would fit the bill. He said they would and stuck a small sticker on the box.

"That was weird," I thought.

I browsed for a few more minutes and saw another brand of insoles that caught my eye. Suddenly, the sales associated reappeared. I showed him the box of insoles I'd just picked up and told him I was thinking of buying them instead of the first pair. Rather than commenting on whether or not I was making a good decision, he said, "Okay, let me get a sticker on that." He put another small sticker on the new box.

I later learned that the store was trying to track how many sales were generated by each associate, and the stickers corresponded to their ID numbers. The store manager had implemented the sticker program in an attempt to better monitor employee performance and learn how to boost sales, but the unintended result was emphasizing ID stickers over customer service. I can imagine the manager contributing to this task focus by issuing frequent reminders: "Don't forget to put your ID sticker on every product you sell so you can get credit for the sale!"

The challenge is that tasks are usually easier to monitor than interactions with customers. It's easy to see if an employee took out the trash, rearranged a display, or put new stock on the sales floor. It's much more difficult to observe whether that employee is providing excellent customer service.

The manager at the sporting goods store would have had to spend more time on the sales floor observing sales associates to see which ones were truly helping customers and exhibiting good sales behaviors. The sticker program was enticing, because it allowed the manager to use a sales report to track performance without ever leaving the office. The blind spot in this system, as was evident from my experience, was that affixing a sticker to an item a customer purchased wasn't necessarily an indicator that an associate had anything to do with generating that sale.

The cure for excessive task orientation is aligning employee responsibilities with the clearly defined customer service culture we discussed in Chapter 3. Employees should be focused on helping customers achieve their goals rather than following a set of rote procedures. Companies can take their service levels to new heights once their employees understand and embrace their role in delivering customer delight.

The Apple Store provides an excellent example of what can happen when employees focus intently on their customers. Unlike many retailers—where employees concentrate on pushing sales, stocking shelves, or ringing up transactions—Apple Store employees are there to create a positive experience for their customers. They conduct product demonstrations, resolve technical problems, and help people get the most out of their MacBook, iPad, or other Apple product. According to Ron Johnson, the former Apple executive who created the Apple Store, every employee has one primary responsibility. "Their job is to figure out what you need and help you get it, even if it's a product Apple doesn't carry."[89]

The results of Apple's customer focus have been impressive. The Apple Store has become widely recognized for its high level of customer service, making the 2018 list of U.S. companies with the best customer service compiled by the American Customer Satisfaction Index (ACSI) and consumer advocate Christopher Elliott.[90] This approach also translates into outstanding financial results: the Apple Store tops all U.S. retailers with an estimated $5,546 in sales per square foot of retail space.[91] (Sales per square foot is a common measure of retail sales efficiency and is obtained by dividing a store's gross revenue by its square footage.)

Employees sometimes struggle to transition from being task-focused to becoming customer-focused, so I've developed a couple of exercises that can be used to change an employee's perspective. The first exercise requires members of a department or team to describe their role from their customers' point of view. In other words, what would you like your customers to say you do for them? Here are a few examples from some of my clients:

- Sales reps at a flower and plant wholesaler decided their role was helping florists (their primary customer) grow their businesses by helping them select flowers and plants that will sell well in their shops.
- Information Technology employees working on a college campus determined that their role was helping faculty and staff minimize downtime due to malfunctioning computers.
- Contact center agents at a medical device manufacturer realized their role was helping to save lives by making sure the right products got to the right doctor in time to help the patients who need them.

The second exercise helps employees integrate this customer focus into their daily activities. Employees start by writing a thank you letter from an imaginary customer, addressing it to themselves. The letter should describe what the employee did and how it helped the customer. Here's an example from when I did the exercise myself:

> Dear Jeff,
>
> Thank you for helping me get my employees obsessed with customer service!
>
> A. Client

Next, ask employees to read their thank you letter at the start of each day for three weeks. They should think about what they would need to do for their customers to feel that way. (You can sign up for a free daily reminder email that includes tips on how to make your thank you letter come to life at toistersolutions.com/thankyou.)

Finally, ask employees to try to receive feedback from a customer that matches their letter. The feedback can be in the form of an actual letter, an email, a response to a survey, or even a verbal compliment. When I was doing this exercise, I emailed a client to check on the progress of an initiative he was working on. I made no mention of my Thank You Letter exercise, but his response was very close to what I had written in my fictitious letter.

He wrote that he'd recently had some success getting his team to buy in on delivering better service, and they'd worked together to identify and resolve an issue that was upsetting some customers. "There is no question in my mind that we are becoming a better company in part because of your teachings," he wrote. "Thank you very much!"

Extreme Role-Playing

In 1971, psychologist Philip G. Zimbardo conducted an experiment at Stanford University to observe the psychology of imprisonment. He recruited 24 male college students who were randomly divided into two groups. Members of one group were designated as prisoners, while members of the other group were the prison guards. The study was intended to take place over the course of two weeks in a mock prison where the guards were instructed to watch over the prisoners.

What happened during the experiment took Zimbardo completely by surprise. Many of the students posing as prison guards soon began engaging in psychologically and even sexually abusive behavior towards the prisoners. Many of the prisoners began to exhibit signs of severe emotional distress. The results were so shocking that the experiment had to be halted after just six days.[92]

Zimbardo's controversial research revealed that ordinarily good people are capable of terrible things when they're put in the wrong environment. These situations start with an adversarial relationship between a group of evildoers and their victims that eventually worsens as people take small steps that unwittingly lead them down a slippery slope of increasingly deplorable behavior. The behavior is allowed to continue because nobody in the group is either willing or able to recognize the path they're on and bring this to the attention of the other members.[93]

I certainly wouldn't put bad customer service on the same plane as the horrible acts that Zimbardo has studied, but his research can help us understand how ordinarily good employees can do terrible things to their customers.

Consider the example of the Transportation Security Administration (TSA). I'm a frequent traveler, and the majority of TSA agents I encounter are friendly and professional. They have a tough job, and most of them seem dedicated to helping provide a safe and efficient travel experience.

Unfortunately, there are a few who subject passengers to rude and unfriendly treatment.

In November 2010, the American Civil Liberties Union received over 900 complaints from passengers who felt their civil rights had been violated by TSA agents. The worst offenders were accused of fondling, groping, and humiliating passengers through the use of new security procedures that had recently been put into effect. The complaints included descriptions of invasive pat-downs that were aggressively carried out in front of other travelers. Some of the complainants were so uncomfortable that they broke down in tears and vowed never to fly again.[94]

How can some TSA agents treat people so horribly? It starts with an "us versus them" approach, where some agents view their primary mission as compliance and crowd control. This effect is enhanced by the uniform and badge worn by TSA agents, which reinforces their position as authority figures.

Many of the TSA agents I come into contact with are polite, professional, and helpful, but I've also witnessed quite a few taking those first few steps down the slippery slope of wrongdoing that Zimbardo describes. These individuals shout at passengers, issue seemingly arbitrary orders, and make demeaning statements about travelers they feel aren't complying quickly enough.

Zimbardo also noted that abuse can flourish when it's passively accepted by members of the group. There have been several other TSA agents present each time I've encountered an abusive agent. The other agents were all within sight and earshot of the agent who was acting out of line, but none of them chose to intervene (at least, not publicly). This sends a clear signal that the agent's inappropriate behavior is condoned, which makes it likely that it will continue.

Another example of inhumane customer treatment is the infamous robo-signer home foreclosure scandal. The scandal erupted in the fall of 2010 when major lenders such as GMAC were accused of employing people who indiscriminately signed off on thousands of foreclosure notices. These employees, dubbed "robo-signers," were approving documents that caused people to lose their homes while shirking their most important responsibility: verifying that no homes were mistakenly foreclosed upon.[95]

Jeffrey Stephan, one of the so-called robo-signers employed by GMAC, gave a deposition in one of the many ensuing lawsuits. His testimony illuminated a mix of factors that contributed to employees like him blindly signing off on thousands of foreclosures. He described how he would sign off on as many as 400 foreclosure notices per day, leaving little time to examine each one. There was no direct contact with homeowners, and Stephan looked solely at the figures presented in the foreclosure notices before signing them, so he was able to take a clinical approach without considering the consequences of his actions. He did his work by following procedures that he was taught through informal training and apparently never questioned what he was being asked to do. From his perspective, it was clear he thought his role was reviewing paperwork and not displacing families from their homes.[96]

TSA and GMAC are extreme examples, but smaller versions exist every day in customer service. There are plenty of employees who have come to believe their role is to stonewall, belittle, or otherwise treat their customers poorly. The lesson from Zimbardo's work is that these employees may not be the inherently bad people we believe them to be. Rather, they are part of an inherently bad system that brings out the worst in people.

Of course, it's also possible for an inherently good system to bring out the best in people. We've described in previous chapters how companies can make it easier for employees to focus on delighting their customers:

- Empower employees to be unreasonably generous to customers. (Chapter 2)
- Create a customer-focused culture. (Chapter 3)
- Put employees in a position where they are intrinsically motivated to do the right thing for their customers. (Chapter 4)
- Eliminate policies that create conflict between customers and employees. (Chapter 5)
- Root out systemic problems that cause poor service. (Chapter 6)
- Make service a priority for all employees. (Chapter 7)

This is a great start, but sometimes employees need a little more help understanding that service comes first. A great example comes from the Transportation and Parking Department at Oregon Health and Science University (OHSU). Like many universities, parking at OHSU is in short supply, so they employ parking enforcement officers who are responsible for patrolling the various parking lots on campus and citing illegally-parked vehicles.

However, the enforcement efforts were creating some customer service headaches. The citations issued generated numerous complaints and were frequently appealed. It got so bad that the department had to assign extra staff to handle the growing backlog of appeals. Even worse, the appeals process resulted in many of the citations being overturned, which meant customers had been needlessly angered and inconvenienced.

Brett Dodson managed the enforcement team and wanted to improve customer service. He knew the key was for his team to spend more time engaging in dialogue with parkers, explaining rules, and providing friendly warnings rather than issuing so many citations. Many of his enforcement officers were having a hard time embracing this vision, though. They relished the opportunity to issue a violation and viewed their role as catching people parking where they shouldn't. A few would even watch someone while they parked illegally and then wait until the driver left the vehicle so they could write a ticket rather than ask that person to park somewhere else.

Dodson decided to try a novel approach. For two months, enforcement officers weren't allowed to issue citations from 8:00 am to 10:00 am each day. These were the hours when most violations traditionally occurred, but Dodson sent his parking enforcement officers out without the handheld computers they needed to issue citations. Their handhelds were returned to them at 10:00, but they were told not to issue a citation unless they had first provided a warning.

It took a couple of months of ongoing effort, but eventually Dodson's work paid off. Most parking enforcement officers learned to gain better compliance by educating parkers and offering alternatives. The number of appealed citations dropped dramatically, freeing up the equivalent of two full-time employees to concentrate on other tasks. Even better, scores on the department's customer satisfaction survey improved dramatically.

Blind Obedience

Philip Zimbardo's research on what makes good people do bad things can be hard for many people to accept. Most of us can't imagine sexually harassing a subject in a psychology experiment, yelling at confused travelers, or unthinkingly signing a document that will cause someone to lose their home. We'd like to believe we would take the high road and question authority when faced with one of those scenarios.

Another prominent psychologist, Stanley Milgram, demonstrated that under the right conditions, the average person will blindly obey an order to do harm. Milgram conducted his classic obedience experiment in 1961, where subjects were instructed to give electric shocks to a person in an adjacent room whenever that person gave an incorrect answer to a memorization test. Unbeknownst to the subject, the person in the other room was actually an actor, and electric shocks weren't really being transmitted. The actor responded to the test questions via a pushbutton device that signaled the answer, but most of the questions were deliberately answered incorrectly.

The initial shocks were a mild 15 volts. The subjects were told to increase the voltage with each incorrect answer by turning a dial on an apparatus that had voltage designations ranging from 15 to 450. When the voltage reached 300, the subject heard the victim banging loudly on the wall of the adjacent room. The victim stopped responding entirely after the voltage reached 315 (labeled "Extreme Intensity Shock" on the dial), but the subjects were told to treat a non-response as an incorrect answer and continue administering the shocks. The shocks continued through 375 volts (labeled "Danger: Severe Shock") and on until the dial reached 450 volts (labeled "XXX").

A whopping 65 percent of the subjects continued administering electric shocks all the way until the voltage reached the maximum 450. Nobody refused to participate in the electric shock experiment after being told about the initial setup and every subject administered at least 300 volts. Only 5 out of 40 subjects stopped their participation in the experiment when they heard the victim banging on the wall.

Most of the subjects became visibly uncomfortable, and many voiced concerns to the person administering the experiment about what they were doing. When subjects displayed signs of reluctance, the experimenter told subjects they must continue, and by and large, they obeyed. These scary results show that people can easily be led to blindly follow directions, even when it should be obvious that those directions will probably result in harm.[97]

Comcast provided a real-world example of how blind obedience can result in ludicrous actions. In July of 2014, Ryan Block called Comcast to cancel his service. Over the course of the call, the employee repeatedly stonewalled Block's cancellation request. Each time Block calmly asked the employee to cancel his service, the employee would reply with a question such as, "Why is it that you're not wanting to have the number one rated internet service?" Block would politely decline to answer the employee's question and again ask to cancel his account. The employee would ignore Block's request and ask another question in an accusatory tone such as, "I'm just trying to figure out here what it is about Comcast's service that you're not liking?"

About 10 minutes into the call, Block began recording the conversation and posted the recording online, where it quickly went viral.[98]

This was not an isolated incident. Complaints about the treatment of customers trying to cancel service had dogged the company for years and continued even after Block posted the recording. (Recall in Chapter 6, where an employee in the same department changed a customer's name to "Asshole Brown" in his account file after the customer's wife had called to cancel a portion of their service.)

The poor treatment administered by Comcast retention specialists was a direct result of the way the company handled account closures. In 2014, customers who wished to cancel their service might start by accessing their account on the Xfinity website, which was the brand name for

Comcast's cable, internet, and phone service. You could quickly make all sorts of adjustments to your account online, including adding new services, but you could not cancel anything. In fact, a notice on the Xfinity website explicitly stated that the company wanted a chance to talk you out of cancelling your service:

> *If you are looking to completely cancel your XFINITY service, we ask that you call us at 1-800-XFINITY (1-800-934-6489). We want to make sure we've done everything we can to give you the best experience, price, and package.*[99]

Customers who called that number were directed to a team of employees called "retention specialists." These employees were specifically trained on techniques to talk customers out of cancelling their service in order to retain their business. They were paid a bonus based on how many customers they talked out of cancelling, and if too many customers were allowed to cancel, an employee's bonus would go to zero.[100]

The retention specialist who spoke with Ryan Block summed up his role perfectly, "My job is to have a conversation with you about keeping your service."

What could happen if a customer service representative thought of disobeying a boss's order because they knew it would result in poor service? If you recall from Chapter 5, employees often weigh the risks and rewards of various options when their employer's poor policies cause them to choose between angering a customer or angering their boss. The risk/reward calculation might still make obedience the most likely option.

Larry (not his real name) worked as a customer service representative for a company in severe financial difficulty. The company was a startup that relied upon independent contractors to serve its clients all over the country. Facing a growing cashflow issue, the company was having a hard time making payments to the contractors. Larry and his coworkers received countless phone calls each day from angry contractors threatening to stop working until their past-due invoices were paid.

The payments weren't coming, but Larry was instructed to lie to contractors so they'd continue working. He was told to blame it on a paperwork error or on some other administrative delay. As a last resort, Larry could transfer the caller into a voicemail box to leave a message for a manager—a manager whom Larry knew wouldn't be returning calls.

Treating contractors this way went against every customer service instinct Larry had, but he dutifully obeyed because disobeying orders could cost Larry his job. He had been unemployed for over a year before he got this position, and he knew how tough the job market was. He considered himself lucky to not be among the employees who were recently laid off. Larry empathized with the unpaid contractors, but he had bills of his own to pay.

If you've read this far in the book, there's a good chance you're genuinely interested in delivering outstanding service. You can't envision yourself or your employees knowingly engaging in abusive acts toward your customers. The good news is that while the research conducted by Philip Zimbardo and Stanley Milgram suggests that otherwise good people are capable of terrible acts when faced with a combination of the wrong conditions, the opposite is also true. You can steer your employees in the proper direction by creating the right conditions for outstanding service.

Many of these steps have already been covered in previous chapters or discussed earlier in this one, so there's no sense in rehashing everything. However, there are three reminders I think are important for customer service leaders.

First, if you look closely at viral service failures, there's usually a company spokesperson who emphatically denies that poor customer treatment is their normal way of doing business. In the immediate aftermath of the David Dao dragging incident (see Chapter 1), United's CEO Oscar Munoz sent an email to employees describing Dao as "disruptive and belligerent" and declaring that employees had "no choice" but to call security to forcibly remove Dao from the plane.[101] John Stumpf, CEO of

Wells Fargo during the company's massive phony account fraud scandal (see Chapter 1), told *The Wall Street Journal*, "There was no incentive to do bad things," and instead blamed a small group of employees who did not reflect the company's culture.[102] And Tom Karinshak, Senior Vice President of Customer Experience at Comcast, released a statement about Ryan Block's phone call that said, "The way in which our representative communicated with him is unacceptable and not consistent with how we train our customer service representatives."

Statements like this tell you that senior management either has no idea what's going on in their own company, or they're distancing themselves from their employees in an effort to find a scapegoat. I was able to review the manual used to train Comcast's retention specialists in 2014, and contrary to Karinshak's statement, the employee was absolutely acting in a way that was consistent with his training. As a leader, you can't avoid service failures if you remain blind to the real challenges that poor products, policies, and procedures create.

In Chapter 5, we discussed how important it is for leaders to have direct contact with customers and frontline employees. Having a genuine understanding of your customers' needs makes it far less likely that you'll ask your employees to carry out an unfair or unfavorable policy. You'll also be more attuned to your employees' behavior and can quickly guide them in the right direction if they get off course.

The second reminder is that leaders must be stewards of the company's customer service culture. As we discussed in Chapter 3, your policies, decisions, and approach to leading others will signal to employees whether or not you're truly committed to customer service. At organizations like the Social Security Administration, TSA, GMAC, or Comcast, the customer was clearly unimportant to senior leaders at that time, or their widespread mistreatment of customers would never have happened. On the other hand, organizations like Apple or OHSU, where service is a priority, usually have results proving they really do care about their customers.

The final reminder is that every leader periodically finds themselves having to prioritize between cost or customers. We'll cover this in greater detail in Chapter 11, but there have been plenty of examples throughout this book where a leader has chosen one over the other. GMAC wouldn't have allowed its employees to cut so many corners in an effort to foreclose on homes as quickly and cheaply as possible if those customers had been important to them, but it happened because company executives were committed to bolstering the bottom line. OHSU wouldn't have foregone so much ticket revenue if they didn't believe it was more important to provide a high level of service to the thousands of faculty, staff, employees, patients, and guests that visited their campus every day.

Customer service leaders have to decide what role they themselves are playing. Is your role keeping service costs to a bare minimum, or is it creating a world-class service organization that helps your business grow by retaining customers?

Solution Summary:
How to Help Employees Establish the Right Roles

As the examples in this chapter illustrate, the service employees provide is often dictated by the role they're playing. Great things can happen when employees understand their primary role is serving customers at the highest level. Getting employees to make that commitment requires a conscious decision and the right working conditions.

Here's a summary of the solutions that can help your customer service representatives make the right choice:

- Align employee responsibilities with your company's service philosophy so employees will naturally deliver outstanding service when they're doing their jobs correctly.
- Have employees write a description of their job describing the value they provide to their customers.

- Use the Thank You Letter exercise to help employees integrate a customer focus into their daily activities.
- Consider extreme measures when necessary to avoid poor customer treatment, such as taking away a Parking Enforcement Officer's ability to write parking tickets so they're compelled to find new ways to achieve results.
- Avoid creating working conditions that could lead employees to subject their customers to poor treatment by maintaining a direct connection to customers and frontline employees, acting as a steward of your organization's customer-focused culture, and understanding when to prioritize service over short-term cost efficiency.

CHAPTER 8 NOTES

86   "Emotional Responses to Tech Support Differs Across Age Groups." Customer Experience Matters blog. November 9, 2017.

87   Tom Anderson. "You may be dead: Every year, Social Security falsely lists 6,000 people as deceased." *CNBC.com.* January 12, 2017.

88   Alex Johnson and Nancy Amons. "Resurrected, but still wallowing in red tape." MSNBC.com. February 29, 2008.

89   Rob Johnson. "What I Learned Building the Apple Store." *Harvard Business Review, HBR Blog Network.* November 21, 2011.

90   Christopher Elliott. "These Companies Have the Best Customer Service." *Forbes.* July 11, 2018.

91   Lauren Thomas. "Bucks from bricks: These retailers make the most money per square foot on their real estate." *CNBC.* July 29, 2017.

92   There is a wealth of information about this study on the Stanford Prison Experiment website: www.prisonexp.org.

93   Philip Zimbardo's presentation at the 2008 TED Conference provides a good overview of his extensive research. "Philip Zimbardo shows how people become monsters... or heroes." http://www.ted.com/index.php/talks/philip_zimbardo_on_the_psychology_of_evil.html.

94   "ACLU reports more than 900 complaints this month over enhanced TSA security measures." American Civil Liberties Union press release. November 24, 2010.

95   David Streitfeld. "Bank of America to Freeze Foreclosure Cases." *The New York Times.* October 1, 2010.

96   Oral deposition of Jeffrey D. Stephan. Maine District Court, District 9. *Federal National Mortgage Association v. Bradbury and GMAC Mortgage, LLC.* June 7, 2010.

97   Stanley Milgram. "Behavioral Study of Obedience." *Journal of Abnormal and Social Psychology.* 67, pgs 371–378. 1963.

98   https://soundcloud.com/ryan-block-10/comcastic-service. Accessed October 5, 2018.

99   xfinity.com. Accessed July 22, 2014.

100 Jeff Toister. "Comcast Botches Service Failure Apology." *Inside Customer Service* blog. July 22, 2014.

101 "United Airlines: Read CEO Oscar Munoz's leaked email to employees in full after passenger dragging incident." *The Independent.* April 11, 2017.

102 Emily Glazer and Christina Rexrode. "Wells Fargo CEO Defends Bank Culture, Lays Blame With Bad Employees." *The Wall Street Journal.* September 13, 2016.

CHAPTER 9

The Problem with Empathy

● ● ●

Encouraging Employees to Empathize with Their Customers

The Cheese Plate Incident is a customer service story that will forever be infamous in my family. It's hard to imagine a plate of cheese causing so much trouble, but the real problem was a lack of empathy that made a simple error comically worse.

My wife and I, along with my parents and in-laws, were staying at a hotel in Phoenix while we were in town to attend a few Spring Training baseball games. One night, the six of us decided to order a meat and cheese plate from room service to have as an appetizer as we all enjoyed a glass of wine before going out to dinner. My wife called to place the order and verified the contents of the meat and cheese plate since a few of us have food allergies. The room service associate told my wife that the meat selection was currently unavailable, but offered to send up a plate of assorted cheeses and crackers instead. My wife agreed to the substitution after making sure it wouldn't trigger anyone's allergies.

A room service attendant arrived with the cheese plate approximately 30 minutes later. Unfortunately, she left the room before we noticed that the assortment also contained salmon, which was a problem because a family member is allergic to seafood. This was puzzling because my wife had specifically mentioned food allergies when she placed the order, and had carefully verified the ingredients to ensure the appetizer would be safe for everyone to enjoy.

I called room service to request a replacement. The hotel associate thought she'd done us a favor by adding the salmon and didn't seem to understand that the salmon could have made someone very ill. She wasn't particularly apologetic, but did agree to send up a cheese plate like the one we'd originally ordered.

We waited another 30 minutes, but the second cheese plate didn't arrive. By now it had been an hour since we placed our original order, and we were getting hungry and impatient. I called room service again and was told our order was delayed because the kitchen had gotten backed up with other orders. The associate promised to send the cheese tray up right away, but it was annoying to have to wait so long since our original order had been incorrect.

Another 15 minutes passed, and still no cheese plate. It would soon be time for us to leave for dinner, so my wife called to see if the cheese plate was on its way. It still hadn't left the kitchen, so she cancelled the order. Once again, the hotel associate wasn't particularly apologetic, but she did agree not to charge us for the appetizer, since they had never delivered the correct order.

The next evening, we returned to our hotel room after a day at the ball park and were surprised to find a plate of cheese and crackers in our room with a note apologizing for the mistake from the night before. Unfortunately, it looked like the plate had been sitting out for quite some time, because the cheese was in bad shape. Even if the cheese plate had been fresh, it would have gone to waste since we were heading straight out to dinner. At that point, all we could do was laugh at how absurd the Cheese Plate Incident had become.

Throughout the experience, our frustration and disappointment arose from a lack of empathy. Adding the salmon to the original order demonstrated that the hotel associate didn't understand our concern about food allergies. Failing to apologize or expedite the replacement showed us she didn't care that we might be irritated by the error—or that we might be hungry! Admitting that the replacement was delayed by other orders told us we weren't a priority. I imagine she thought she'd recovered by sending us a cheese plate and an apology card the following evening, but in reality, it felt like salt on the wound because it went to waste.

In this chapter, we'll see that service failures like the Cheese Plate Incident often happen because empathy is a difficult skill for employees to master. Many employees lack the fundamental experiences upon which empathy is built. They find it hard to understand their customers' emotions, or they fail to grasp the importance of addressing these emotions when a service failure occurs. They may not even realize that their customers' perspective is different from their own and miss out on opportunities to serve because they only see the world through their own eyes.

The good news is that customer service representatives can learn to be more empathetic, but it involves careful training and a patient supervisor.

The Source of Empathy

Empathy is a customer service skill that helps people avoid situations like the Cheese Plate Incident by seeing things from their customers' perspective. It helps them understand how the customer is thinking and feeling in a given situation, and take steps to ensure the customer is satisfied. Without empathy, employees may see problems differently than their customers, or perhaps not see the problems at all.

The ability to empathize with another person comes from having had a similar or closely-related experience. You're able to understand what the other person is thinking and feeling, because you've been there yourself or you've experienced something that was close enough. For example, if you've ever accidentally touched a hot iron, you're likely to wince if you see someone accidentally touch a hot stove.[103]

Many employees struggle to empathize with customers because they don't have a similar experience they can relate to. An accountant probably does their own taxes, so they may not understand the confusion their clients experience when they try to fill out tax forms. A person answering a tech support hotline likely fixes their own computer, so they might have trouble understanding the helplessness customers feel when their computers stop working. There's a good chance that a valet parking a $100,000 sports car doesn't understand the anxiety a customer feels when entrusting something so expensive to a stranger.

A lack of related experience might have been one of the causes of the Cheese Plate Incident. The guest service associate may not have realized that seafood is a common allergen if she didn't have food allergies herself. She might not have understood that the replacement cheese plate needed to be expedited if she didn't have the experience to know hotel guests ordering appetizers are likely to have other plans that evening. When she had a replacement cheese plate delivered the next day, it probably wouldn't occur to her that we might not be there to enjoy it if she didn't travel often enough to understand that guests don't always keep the same schedule.

Perhaps what's most confounding about empathy is how obvious the problem seems to those of us who *can* relate to the situation. Employees who have had similar experiences are often naturally able to empathize with their customers in a way that other employees can't. I frequently see young mothers traveling on airplanes with fussy infants, and the most helpful flight attendants are consistently those who are mothers themselves. They understand the difficulties of traveling with an infant and are able tell the young mother, "Here's what I did when my kids were that age."

The easiest customers to serve are frequently people who have worked in similar positions and can empathize with the employee who is assisting them. Friends of mine who spent years working as food servers always make a point to tip generously, because they know tips are an important part of a server's income. People who have worked in contact centers often try to be extra polite and patient with the person on the other end of the line, because they understand how stressful the job can be. When I try on clothes in a store, I always clear out my dressing room, because clearing out dressing rooms was the chore I enjoyed least when I worked in retail.

If empathy comes from having had similar experiences, the easiest way to help customer service employees become more empathetic is to put them in their customers' shoes.

One way to do this is by having employees experience your product or service as a customer. At the USS Midway Museum in San Diego, every new employee takes the museum tour so they have the experience of being a visitor. At LinkedIn Learning (a company I'm affiliated with through my training videos), the sales team reported having its best quarter ever after taking more of the online courses they were selling to clients.[104] Airbnb gives employees travel credit so they can stay in homes owned by Airbnb hosts when they travel.

Another way to put employees in their customers' shoes is through sharing personal stories from customers. Stories are a powerful way of tapping into our imagination and helping us understand how the characters may have felt or what they were thinking. I've worked with several clients who make medical devices, and they all use a similar technique to help employees empathize with their customers. Throughout these companies' offices, you'll find posters picturing real patients who have been helped by their products. Each poster offers a brief description of a patient's disease or injury and explains how a particular product helped improve or even save their life.

These examples remind employees of the importance of what they're doing. And even if they don't have direct patient contact, they go to work each day knowing they're positively impacting other people's lives. In many cases, the stories also remind employees of a friend or family member who faced a similar medical ordeal.

A third option is to hire employees who already have similar experiences to the customers they'll be serving. One of the reasons I enjoy shopping at the sporting goods retailer REI is that their employees tend to be avid users of the equipment they sell. When my wife and I went there to buy backpacks for a hiking trip, the associate who helped us was an experienced backpacker who understood the nervousness of planning a first-time wilderness expedition. He helped us select the right gear, and more important, he took extra time to reassure us about our plans.

Communicating on Different Levels

Empathy can also be a challenge because customers and customer service representatives often rely on different parts of their brain as they communicate with each other.

Customers tend to engage the part of the brain that regulates emotion, especially when they feel something is going wrong. A 2011 study by Bård Tronvol, published in the *Journal of Service Management*, found that 97 percent of customers feel negative emotions such as frustration, anger, or helplessness when they experience a service failure.[105] From the customer's perspective, empathizing with negative emotions is an important part of the solution when a service failure is being addressed.

Unfortunately, negative emotions often go undetected or unacknowledged by employees who are focused on finding a rational solution to their customer's problem. Without empathy, employees will have a hard time understanding how their customer is feeling, because rational thinking and emotions are controlled by two separate parts of our brain. The customer service rep isn't experiencing the customer's emotions, so it's easier for them to engage the part of the brain that regulates rational thinking as they try to deliver service.[106]

I received an email with a discount offer from an online shoe retailer, and it happened to be time for me to buy some new running shoes. I clicked on the email link, went to the website, and picked out a pair.

However, my promised discount wasn't deducted from my order total. I still wanted the shoes, so I sent an email to their customer service department to see if someone could help me complete my order and apply the discount.

The next day, I received a response from Adam in the customer service department. He told me that I would have to call the company's toll-free hotline and place my order over the phone with a customer service representative. Adam reminded me to explain the situation and told me the rep would honor the promotion.

Adam was clearly communicating with me on a rational level. From that perspective, my problem was solved. I needed to know how to take advantage of the promotion when placing my order, and he had provided that information.

But Adam's response did little to make me feel better about the experience. I was frustrated by the initial problem. Now I was annoyed by the additional hassle of having to call their customer service department. I was also irritated that Adam had passed my problem off to someone else.

Fortunately, the opposite experience occurred when I called the customer service line to place my order. The customer service rep, Laura, was friendly and apologetic, and her empathetic response to my situation instantly made me feel better. While placing the order, I told Laura that I was going to be out of town in a few days and was concerned that my shoes would be delivered while I was away. She assured me that she understood and would make sure the delivery was timed to arrive on a day when I would be home to receive it. To my surprise, my shoes arrived just two days later. Laura had upgraded my shipping to express delivery at no extra charge. Her empathetic approach turned a negative experience into a very positive one.

Why did Laura succeed where Adam failed? While Adam simply provided information, Laura addressed how I felt. She acknowledged and apologized for my frustration. She instilled confidence that she'd be able to handle the situation with minimal hassle. Best of all, she understood my concerns about having a package sitting on my doorstep while I was out of town and took steps to ensure that didn't happen.

Service failures occur every day when employees offer rational solutions without addressing their customers' underlying emotions. A restaurant manager who offers a free dessert when a customer complains about too much dressing on their salad may embarrass someone who is watching their weight. They'd likely get better results by offering a sincere apology and expediting a replacement salad with the dressing on the side so the customer could add it according to their liking. An appliance repair technician might think they did a great job when they get their customer's washing machine running again, but may not notice the customer is irritated that they arrived 45 minutes late. The repair technician could make a better recovery by empathizing with the inconvenience the customer suffered from a late service call on top of a broken appliance, and apologize profusely. A doctor who prescribes a routine blood test may add to a patient's anxiety if they don't sense the patient's nervousness about what the test results could reveal. The doctor would make the patient feel much better if they took a few moments to explain the purpose of the tests and offer a realistic view of what the results might indicate.

According to psychologist Guy Winch, we often experience a need to have our emotions validated when we get angry or upset. We want the other person to understand why we feel the way we do and to acknowledge that our feelings are reasonable given the situation. Having our emotions validated can bring instant relief and make us feel better.[107]

Customers who experience a problem may get even more upset when their emotions aren't validated or their feelings are ignored, such as when a customer service rep focuses on providing a rational solution to a problem without sincerely apologizing. These situations highlight how customers and employees often communicate on different levels, with the customer getting angrier due to a lack of empathy and the employee getting confused by a customer who seems to get more irate the more they try to provide a solution.

Chapter 2 discussed ways that unreasonable customers can be an obstacle to outstanding service. One of the reasons customers become unreasonable is that the emotional part of our brain has the ability to hijack rational thinking. Exceptionally strong emotions—such as frustration, anger, or even shame—can cloud our ability to reason and impair our judgment.

This means that taking a rational approach to an extremely upset customer can be like pouring gas on a fire. I once watched a hotel guest fly off the handle when he tried to check in to the hotel and was told he had no reservation and that the hotel was sold out for the evening. He insisted he had a confirmed reservation and demanded that the hotel find him a room. The guest started yelling at the front desk associate and slamming his hand on the counter as his frustration steadily increased.

The front desk associate made the mistake of focusing on rational solutions rather than first diffusing the guest's extreme anger. She suggested that an error might have been made when the guest made his reservation, but this just made him more furious. The guest yelled even louder when the associate offered to accommodate him at a nearby hotel. A manager finally stepped in to address the situation, and made things worse by telling the man, "Sir, I'm going to have to ask you to calm down." This made the guest so irate that the hotel's security officer had to intervene.

The front desk associate at the hotel could have defused the situation by taking a moment to empathize with a tired and frustrated traveler. Rather than trying to prove the guest was wrong and she was right, she could have started the discussion by apologizing for the situation and indicating that he was perfectly right to feel frustrated. She shouldn't have continued to offer solutions until she could help the guest overcome his initial surprise and anger. If he was still extremely agitated, the associate could then call her manager over to speak privately with the guest and find a solution.

Customer service employees can learn to identify and address their customers' emotional needs in situations like this, but this should never be left to chance. It takes training and practice to help employees empathize with their customers. There are also some things you simply have to experience to learn, such as the fact that telling an irate customer to calm down will almost certainly have the opposite effect!

Here's a simple exercise you can use to help employees develop their empathy skills. Start by picking a situation where your customers are likely to get angry, upset, or confused. For example, employees in a furniture store may find that customers are disappointed or frustrated if a piece of furniture they ordered doesn't arrive by the expected delivery date.

Next, have employees think of a situation when they encountered a similar problem and ask them to describe how they felt when it happened. The furniture store employees might recall a time when they ordered something that didn't arrive on time, which could be anything from a piece of furniture to a pizza. Typical emotions they experienced as a result could include disappointment, frustration, and even anger if the delay caused additional inconvenience.

Finally, help employees brainstorm ways they can help customers avoid experiencing similar emotions. This exercise might help the furniture store employees realize that a sincere and heartfelt apology is necessary when an order is delayed. They may need to bend the rules to offer a more precise delivery time than the four-hour window called for by company policy to make up for the inconvenience caused by the delay. Or perhaps they can discount or waive the delivery fee to make it up to the customer.

Another technique employees can use to neutralize negative emotions is called the "preemptive acknowledgement." This technique involves identifying a situation that may lead to a customer's negative emotions *before* the customer gets upset. The preemptive acknowledgement allows an employee to acknowledge a service failure and suggest a solution without the customer ever becoming angry.

Here's a scenario we've all experienced that highlights how powerful the preemptive acknowledgement can be. Imagine you are dining at a busy restaurant. You and your party place your orders and engage in lively conversation while waiting for your dinner. After a while, your growling stomach reminds you that it's taking a long time for your meal to arrive. You notice your water glass is empty and then realize the people at the table next to you are enjoying their food, even though they were seated 10 minutes after you were. To make matters worse, you have to flag down another server to get an update since yours is suddenly nowhere to be found. Everyone at the table is irritated by the time the food finally arrives.

Now let's look at the same situation where your server uses the preemptive acknowledgement. You're dining at a busy restaurant and enjoying lively conversation after placing your order. After a while, your growling stomach reminds you that it's taking a long time for your food to arrive. Just then, your server arrives at your table and politely interrupts your conversation.

"I'm so sorry for the delay. I just checked with the kitchen, and your order is the next one up. In the meantime, may I refill your drinks?"

Everyone at the table thanks your server for checking in and refilling their drinks. The server returns a few minutes later with everyone's food. The short delay is completely forgotten as you enjoy your meal.

The preemptive acknowledgement is effective, because it prevents customers' negative emotions from hijacking their rational thinking. A meal that takes 10 minutes too long to arrive hardly qualifies as the worst customer service ever, but an emotional cocktail of hunger, irritation, and a sense of unfair treatment can make it seem that way. Avoiding these strong emotions allows customers to keep their good humor and maintain an appropriate perspective.

Training employees to use the preemptive acknowledgement has the extra benefit of helping them become more observant of their customers' needs. By paying close attention and learning to be more observant, a restaurant server will realize when a table of customers has waited too long for their meal. This realization prompts them to check on the order in the kitchen, which in turn allows them to apologize to the guests for the delay and provide an update.

Self-Centered Behavior that Leads to Poor Service

Expressing empathy requires us to view things from the other person's perspective, but this can be challenging because our natural perspective is our own.

Many of us rarely use cash to pay for purchases these days, but notice what happens the next time you do and the cashier hands you your change. Do they put the bills in your palm with the coins on top, making it hard for you to grab the loose coins? Or do they put the coins in your palm first, and then place the bills on top?

Most cashiers will collect the coins from their register first and then grab the necessary bills while the coins sit in the palm of their hand. It's easier to do it this way, because coins are harder to pick up when you have a handful of bills. If the casher simply turns their hand over to place the change in the customer's hand, the bills will be in the customer's palm and the coins will sit on top of the bills. It's a very efficient maneuver, but it also makes the coins harder for the customer to corral.

Some cashiers realize that if it's difficult for them to hold coins on top of the bills in their hand, it will be difficult for their customers too. They place the coins in their customer's palm first and then the bills on top. It takes the slightest bit of extra effort, but the result is that customers spend less time fumbling with their change or dropping coins.

Using empathy to see things from a customer's perspective can be difficult under normal circumstances, but it becomes extremely tough for customer service employees when their own emotions are running high. My wife and I experienced this while vacationing in San Francisco when we visited a bar that had been recommended by several friends. The bar was packed when we arrived, and we were fortunate to snag the last open table. When our server finally made it over to take our drink order, we could tell by the look on her face that she was overwhelmed by the crowd.

Our server returned about 20 minutes later and brusquely dropped two drinks on our table. Unfortunately, they weren't our drinks. "Excuse me," I said. "I don't think this is what we ordered."

The server looked at the drinks and then exclaimed, "Aw shit!"

We sat in stunned silence as she scooped up the drinks without saying another word. It took another 20 minutes for her to return with our correct order. She put the drinks on our table and quickly left without apologizing for the error, the delay, or her exclamation.

This server's customer service was inexcusable, but we could do our own empathy exercise to better understand her behavior. Think of a time when you felt overwhelmed by work and were so busy you barely had time to think. You probably developed a sort of tunnel vision, where you blocked out all other distractions so you could focus on the unending tasks at hand. I know when I experience this I'm able to accomplish more work, yet I also become more abrupt with the people around me.

Now think about our bar server. If she was experiencing this type of stress-induced tunnel vision, it was probably a major setback for her to find out she delivered an incorrect drink order to our table. Her natural inclination would be to feel even more stress—and perhaps a little helpless—when she discovered she'd need to make an extra trip to the bar to correct our order. Our mild disappointment at being served the wrong drinks had no chance of showing up on her radar.

This type of scenario is often at the core of really bad customer service. The customer feels some type of negative emotion due to a service failure, but the employee doesn't acknowledge the customer's feelings because they're experiencing their own negative emotions. This causes the customer to get even more upset, because they're confronted with a bad employee attitude rather than the validation they needed.

Chapter 6 revealed ways that poor products, processes, and procedures can contribute to employee dissatisfaction. A company that has these types of chronic service failures will find it difficult to have empathetic customer service representatives. Over time, the employees' own feelings of frustration and helplessness—arising from repeatedly handling the same problems—will cause them to stop observing or caring about their customers' feelings.

Companies that are going out of business provide a prime example of what can happen when employees' emotions make it hard for them to serve their customers. When the book retailer Borders announced in July 2011 that they were closing their stores and liquidating the company, a change happened among many of its employees. Suddenly faced with the prospect of losing their jobs, associates decided to let their customers know how they really felt. A much publicized example was provided by employees at the Borders in Mansfield, Massachusetts, who posted a handwritten sign titled, "Things we never told you: ode to a bookstore death." The sign listed 16 grievances about their customers, including questions they thought were stupid, gripes about their customers' tastes in literature, and complaints about customers' shopping habits.[108]

In any situation, overcoming the obstacle of empathy requires a solution that adopts the customer's perspective at the employee, managerial, and organizational levels.

At the employee level, training must be provided to help people understand the customer's point of view. For instance, a cashier should be trained to give change by first putting the coins in their customer's hand and then placing the bills on top. This was the first lesson I learned when I was trained to be a cashier, and no doubt it would have taken me a long time to learn it on my own if my trainer hadn't emphasized its importance.

At the managerial level, customer service supervisors must empathize with their employees, as well as with their customers. They must understand that providing service can sometimes cause frustration, irritation, and other negative emotions. Leaders who fail to recognize their employees' emotions run the risk of having those emotions hijack their employees' ability to empathize with customers.

When I was a customer service manager, I learned that it was important to let my reps vent for a few minutes after working with a particularly difficult customer. This let them get it off their chest without taking it out on the next person they served. It also let my employees know I acknowledged their feelings. The catch was that I insisted that we end the conversation by discussing strategies for dealing with similar customers in the future so my employees could learn from their experiences.

On an organizational level, companies need to work to eliminate sources of employee angst that might make it hard for them to empathize with customers. This includes the products, processes, and procedures discussed in Chapter 6 that systematically result in poor service. For example, if the bar in San Francisco I visited with my wife was chronically understaffed, they would need to hire and train more capable servers to work each shift or risk burning out their employees and turning away customers who experienced slow and surly service.

Solution Summary:
Helping Employees Demonstrate Empathy with Customers

Empathy doesn't always come naturally to employees, but they can learn to understand and validate their customers' emotions. Here's a short summary of the solutions presented in this chapter:

- Help your employees develop relevant, related experiences they can use to empathize with customers, such as giving them the opportunity to be a customer themselves.
- Share stories and testimonials from real customers to remind your employees how great service can make their customers feel understood and acknowledged.
- Hire employees who use your product or service so they can easily relate to the people they serve.

- Train employees to understand how customers feel when they encounter a problem by asking employees to recall a similar experience. Have them describe how the experience made them feel, and then discuss ways they can help their customers avoid those feelings.
- Teach employees to use the preemptive acknowledgement to defuse customers' negative emotions before they explode.
- Show employees how to deliver service from their customers' perspective, such as the correct way to hand change to a customer.
- Demonstrate empathy toward employees when they experience negative emotions to validate their feelings and prevent them from taking out their frustrations on a customer.
- Eliminate the sources of employee angst that could cause them to fail to identify and react to their customers' negative emotions.

CHAPTER 9 NOTES

103 Jean Decety and Philip L. Jackson. "A Social-Neuroscience Perspective on Empathy." *Current Directions in Psychological Science*, Vol. 15, No 2. Association for Psychological Science, 2006.

104 John Abrams. "We Just Had our Best Sales Quarter Ever. Our Secret? A 17x Increase in eLearning." *LinkedIn Learning* blog. March 12, 2018.

105 Bård Tronvoll. "Negative Emotions and Their Effect on Customer Complaint Behaviour." *Journal of Service Management*, 22(1), pgs 111–134. 2011.

106 Daniel Goleman. *Working with Emotional Intelligence*. Bantam Books. New York, 1998.

107 Guy Winch. "The Antidote to Anger and Frustration." *Psychology Today. Squeaky Wheel* blog. June 18, 2011.

108 Patrick Anderson. "Borders Gets the Last Word." *The Sun Chronicle*. Attleboro, MA. September 22, 2011.

CHAPTER 10

Emotional Roadblocks

• • •

Helping Employees Manage Their Own Emotions

One of my lowest moments in customer service was when I deliberately hung up on a customer, knowing full well that if she called back and asked to speak to the manager, she would get me on the phone once again.

It wasn't the right way to handle things—and I learned from the experience—but in that particular moment, I let my emotions get the best of me. It wasn't really that specific customer that set me off. A swirl of negative emotions had been building for quite some time, and this person was just the spark that ignited the blaze.

For starters, I didn't like my job. I had accepted the position as the Customer Service Manager for a small catalog company six months prior, because my wife and I were moving to San Diego from Boston. I moved out first to get a job so we'd have at least one income as we settled into our new home town. It was the best job I could get in the three weeks budgeted for my job search, but I wouldn't otherwise have chosen to work for this company. Even during the interview process, I'd had the sense it was going to be a difficult place to work.

If you've ever had a bad boss, you know how hard it can be to go to work each day. I had two bad bosses: the company's owners, who were the president and CFO. They didn't communicate well and often gave conflicting orders that pulled me in different directions, so I was constantly confused about my job responsibilities and main priorities. The president was particularly unfriendly and angered easily.

The day I hung up on the customer was a week before Christmas. A perfect storm of three problems converged to cause a deluge of angry calls that went far beyond what you'd expect during the normal holiday rush.

First, many of our most popular items were backordered, and our supplier had just informed us that a delivery that would have allowed us to fill a lot of orders would not arrive before Christmas as we had expected. Second, major blizzards throughout the country had caused many shipments to be delayed or lost. Third, poor process control in our warehouse contributed to an extraordinarily high number of shipping errors, where packages were sent with the wrong item or to the wrong address. My whole team was working long hours and facing an enormous amount of stress.

On this particular day, I'd already spent eight hours on the phone because we were drowning in calls. An alarm would sound throughout the entire company whenever a customer was on hold for more than a minute, and everyone in the company was expected to answer the phones when the alarm went off. My coworkers in other departments were frustrated with me, because they'd had to spend much of their day on the phone instead of doing their normal work. The president wouldn't allow me to change the alarm setting to keep customers on hold longer before it sounded off, but that day he'd been sending me angry emails because he too, was spending a chunk of his day on the phone. However, I was completely powerless to stop the flood of callers.

I finally hit my boiling point with one particular customer. She was yelling insults at me as I tried in vain to apologize and find a solution. *Click.* I hung up.

I'm not proud of my actions in that moment, but I'm grateful for the experience, because it helped me fully understand how difficult customer service can be. Everyone who's spent more than a few days in customer service has had experiences where they felt angry, frustrated, and helpless. After all, we're all human!

In this chapter, we'll look at ways employees' emotions can negatively affect their performance. We'll see how our instinctive reaction when someone is yelling at us can easily lead to poor service. We'll discover that negative emotions are contagious and can spread from customers to employees. Finally, we'll examine how difficult it can be to smile when we just don't feel like smiling.

Companies that are committed to outstanding service must make it easy for their employees to be happy and help employees develop skills to work through situations when they experience the negative emotions that come with the job.

"Don't Take It Personally" Is Bad Advice

I can't count how many times I've heard someone say "Don't take it personally" to an employee who's upset after working with a difficult customer. I'm sure I've said it myself a few times. You may have had the same thought about me as you read my story at the beginning of this chapter.

But our natural instinct is to take things personally when someone is directing their anger or frustration at us. Called the "fight or flight response," symptoms include dilated pupils, trembling, flushed skin, faster breathing, and a racing heartbeat.[109] We're likely to feel emotions such as anger, embarrassment, or even fear that can cause us to lash out at the other person or find a way to retreat.

The challenge in a customer service setting is that we're expected to counter that basic fight or flight instinct and instead keep calm, remain friendly, and try to help the other person. Expecting someone to dismiss this normal reaction is like telling them not to laugh when they hear a funny joke or not to be concerned when they learn a family member has lost their job. It takes effort and training for employees to learn to manage their emotional reactions.

For another explanation as to why serving upset customers is so difficult, it's helpful to turn to the work of Abraham Maslow, a psychologist famous for developing a list of factors that motivate people, often referred to as Maslow's hierarchy of human needs. This framework describes our basic motivators in priority order, where the first priority must be satisfied before we can be motivated by the next priority. For example, humans have a strong desire to be safe from physical harm, but someone who has unmet physiological needs such food, water, or sleep would be willing to put their safety at risk in an effort to survive.[110] Here is Maslow's list in priority order:

1. Physiological
2. Safety
3. Love and Belonging
4. Esteem
5. Self-Actualization

I've trained thousands of customer service employees, and nearly all of them have a strong desire to be good at what they do. This intent fits squarely with self-actualization, which means the ability to perform at the peak of one's abilities. However, people are only motivated to be the best they can be when all their higher-priority needs are being met. A customer directing a verbal tirade at an employee challenges the employee's self-esteem, so that the employee's motivation to help the upset customer becomes a lower priority than the need to protect their self-esteem.

For example, here's a story from Paul, who was working in the office at a night club when he received a phone call from a customer who was upset because his credit card company had detected a fraudulent charge.

The customer was convinced that a server at the club had stolen his credit card number. At first, Paul tried his best to be helpful, but he quickly realized the man just wanted to vent. The customer's repeated accusations of "Your server stole my credit card number" and "You guys need to be more careful" soon wore thin.

Paul explained how he experienced the fight or flight response. "I could feel my blood pressure going up. I could feel my face get flush. I felt like, 'Don't accuse my coworker of doing something that you don't know that they did. There was a million ways that credit card numbers get stolen. It was so frustrating to me."

The customer's uncooperative approach made it hard for Paul to manage his emotions despite his years of experience in the hospitality industry. It was insulting to hear the customer accuse his coworker of a crime without providing a shred of evidence. The caller repeatedly used the word *you*, which could have meant "the club," but it was hard for Paul to avoid feeling like it was a personal attack.

Towards the end of the call, Paul stopped worrying about helping the customer. "I got to the point where I was so done with him. I started doing everything I could to get him off the phone."

Working with upset customers is difficult, but it gets even harder for employees to manage their emotions when they have a boss or coworkers who are unsupportive. The social structure provided by the workplace is a powerful part of most employees' lives, and it's often noted that we spend more time with our coworkers than we do with our own families. This makes it vitally important that we have a sense of belonging at work, since—according to Maslow's hierarchy—the human desire for love and acceptance is a more powerful motivator than esteem or self-actualization.

The day I hung up on my customer, I was having a hard time managing my emotions because two important needs weren't being met. The customer's tirade challenged my sense of self-esteem and frustrated me because I felt she was more interested in insulting me than in letting me try to assist her. Even worse, I was affected by a toxic work environment at a job I couldn't stand, a boss who was angry at me for reasons I felt were his own doing, and coworkers who were frustrated with me, too. I experienced no sense of belonging during that moment, and I had suddenly stopped caring about whether or not I did a good job.

A 2011 study by researchers at Bowling Green State University found a correlation between employee performance and the extent to which employees are subjected to mistreatment from customers and coworkers. The study, which focused on bank tellers at a regional bank, found that tellers who reported high levels of customer and coworker incivility were absent from work at least one more day per month than their colleagues. These same employees also experienced a 13 percent decrease in sales performance (opening new accounts and selling additional products to customers).[111]

Clearly, companies need to offer their employees more than pithy advice to help them avoid resorting to poor service when confronted by an angry or upset customer. Employees need a supportive work environment that encourages their commitment to the team. They must also be helped to develop the skills they need to handle upset customers more effectively.

Companies that consistently deliver outstanding service base their success on a counterintuitive approach: they emphasize that employees, not customers, are most important. In Chapter 2, we discussed the importance of protecting employees from abusive customers as a way to encourage loyalty and commitment. Putting employees first promotes a sense of belonging and high self-esteem that ultimately leads to more positive relationships with both customers and coworkers.

Southwest Airlines is an example of a company that embraces an employee-first philosophy. The company's founder, Herb Kelleher, described the importance of this strategy in an interview with CNBC. "Employees first, customers second, shareholders third. If the employees serve the customer well, the customer comes back, and that makes the shareholders happy. It's simple, it's not a conflict, it's a chain. If you treat-ed the employees well, if you cared for them, if you value them as people, if you gave them psychic satisfaction in their jobs, then they would really do a great job for the customers and the customers would come back, which would be good for the shareholders."[112]

Of course, all customer service employees will occasionally encoun-ter a customer whose anger is hard to handle. Effective customer service leaders keep in mind how difficult it is for employees to manage their emotions in these situations. An employee who is giving their best effort will benefit from a supervisor who helps them approach a customer ser-vice incident as a learning experience rather than a reason for disciplinary action. A leader who's too quick to punish employees who give honest effort will likely lose their respect, so punitive measures such as written warnings, suspensions, and terminations are best reserved for willful acts of egregiously poor service, disastrous lapses in judgment, or an inability to learn from repeated mistakes.

There are three things that supervisors can do to help their employees learn from experience and improve their ability to manage their emotions in stressful situations. First, the supervisor should help the employee evaluate the situation and determine why the customer was angry. The intent isn't to place blame, but rather to diagnose the root cause.

Second, the supervisor and employee should discuss strategies for getting better results when the employee encounters a similar situation in the future. Could the employee do or say something a little differently? Is there an opportunity to defuse the customer's anger before it boils over?

Finally, the supervisor should encourage the employee to apply these new strategies on the job.

This supportive approach will make employees more likely to be forthcoming, asking their supervisor for help rather than trying to prevent the boss from hearing about an incident with a difficult customer. It also fosters a spirit of continuous improvement, where employees get better and better at handling difficult situations over time.

Emotions Are Contagious

For customer service employees, the job is even more challenging because emotions are contagious. An encounter with an angry customer can leave the employee feeling irritable, and that feeling can linger as they interact with other customers. Likewise, a particularly outgoing customer can make the employee feel upbeat and help them deliver a higher level of service to people they subsequently encounter.[113]

Looking back at that inglorious day when I hung up on a customer, I now understand how contagious emotions played a role in my actions. It seemed like I was receiving anger from all sides. My boss was angry at me, my coworkers were annoyed with me, and my customers were furious. I was becoming angrier and angrier myself with each person I encountered. This anger reached its apex with the customer who wouldn't stop insulting me.

It may be tempting to observe situations like mine and think that customer service employees should simply resist getting infected with other people's emotions. Unfortunately, the contagious effects of other people's emotions are often experienced unconsciously. An employee might not realize an upset customer is making them angry until the anger begins to impair their ability to provide good customer service.

In 2000, researchers at Uppsala University in Sweden published the results of an experiment that confirmed how people can unconsciously react to emotions expressed by others. Subjects in the experiment were either exposed to images of people who were smiling or who looked angry. These images were visible for just 30 milliseconds, which is too short a time for the conscious brain to notice the image, but long enough for the unconscious brain to process it. The happy or angry pictures were closely followed by an image of someone with a neutral expression that was displayed for five seconds. Throughout the experiment, subjects were connected to tiny electrodes that allowed the experimenters to measure the subjects' facial reactions.

The electrodes detected facial movements in the subjects that aligned with the pictures they were unconsciously exposed to. The group who saw images of people smiling displayed a higher level of activity in the muscles used to smile, while the group who saw pictures of angry people had a higher level of activity in the muscles that create a frown. None of the subjects were aware of seeing the happy or angry faces when they were debriefed after the experiment.[114]

You can have a little fun conducting your own version of this experiment by smiling at strangers in public. This works particularly well in a crowded area where many people are passing by, such as an airport or a shopping mall. Try to make eye contact and smile at people as they pass by, and you'll be amazed at how many complete strangers automatically smile back.

Contagious negative emotions don't come exclusively from customers, bosses, and coworkers. Factors outside the work environment can influence employees' emotions. Personal problems—such as an argument with a spouse, a sick child, or financial difficulties—can all contribute to a sour mood. Something as simple as an inconsiderate driver during an employee's morning commute can infect that employee's state of mind.

Companies that offer outstanding service strive to make their work environments as positive as possible. Positive emotions are just as contagious as negative feelings, and upbeat employees lead to happier customers and coworkers in a self-reinforcing cycle. These organizations foster an enjoyable work environment by helping employees create strong bonds with their coworkers, bosses, and the company as a whole.

Encouraging friendships among coworkers is an important first step. According to a 2014 study by the human resources software company Globoforce, employees who counted between one to five coworkers as friends were nearly twice as likely to be proud of their company as employees who had no friends at work. And employees with 25 or more friends at work were more than three times as likely to be proud of their company as employees who did not have coworker friends.[115]

Employees naturally provide better service when they take pride in their company. Friends also make it easier for employees to keep their spirits high and to recover from negative situations, such as an angry customer.

Of course, friendships at work must form naturally, but companies can influence their development through a variety of strategies. Here are a few examples.

- Holding informal social events after work encourages employees to interact with each other in a casual setting.
- Varying work schedules and project assignments gives people the opportunity to work with a variety of coworkers.
- Hiring new employees in groups or "cohorts" helps them become friendly with each other as they go through the experience of being a new employee.

Bosses can also play a big role in helping employees maintain a positive frame of mind. A supportive supervisor helps employees recover quickly from encounters with difficult customers. On the other hand, an unfriendly boss generates negative emotions that tend to lead to poor service.

Supervisors need supervision, too. Executives need to be in tune with employees two or more levels below them so they understand the impact supervisors are having on morale. Senior leaders in customer-focused companies often spend time creating relationships with frontline employees and coaching managers and supervisors on how to continuously improve their leadership skills. These executives also watch out for the warning signs of a potentially negative manager, such as abnormally high turnover, poor customer service ratings, or even employee complaints.

This leads to the third level of responsibility: senior executives need to make the company a place where employees want to work. It should be seen as a refuge, so even those employees experiencing personal problems can feel as though their burden is lifted when they come to work.

In her book, *The Good Jobs Strategy*, Massachusetts Institute of Technology professor Zeynep Ton details how leading customer-centric companies such as Costco, QuikTrip, and Trader Joe's thrive in low-margin businesses by investing more in their employees. These organizations offer a better package of compensation, benefits, and other perks than competitors, because they understand the benefits of attracting top talent, having low turnover, and encouraging loyalty and productivity. Most important, employees feel a sense of pride in their work and understand the value of their contributions to the company's success.[116]

The High Cost of Emotional Labor

Most customer service positions have standards governing the emotions that employees should express to their customers. These standards, called "display rules," include typical service behaviors such as making eye contact, smiling, and addressing people with a warm and friendly tone. They may be explicitly defined in a procedure or a set of customer service standards, or implicitly expected as part of our cultural norms for customer service professionals.

Display rules are easy to follow when they're in sync with our genuine emotions. Smiling, making eye contact, and warmly addressing customers come naturally when we're in a good mood. However, these same rules can be exceedingly difficult to follow when our true emotions don't match. An employee who's experiencing anger, sadness, or frustration is still expected to smile at customers, but it's very hard to make that smile appear genuine.

Customers are usually able to perceive the difference between sincere expressions of emotion and employees who are engaged in what's called "surface acting," where the displayed emotion doesn't match their true feelings.[117] The airline industry is often cited as an example where there can be a stark contrast between the expected display rules and how flight attendants actually feel. Pacific Southwest Airlines even played to this notion when they ran a funny ad campaign in 1979 called "Our smiles aren't just painted on" that emphasized their authentic service in contrast to competitors' disingenuous attempts to appear friendly.[118]

As a frequent traveler, I often have the chance to observe the gap between flight attendants' real and displayed feelings. I can overhear their candid conversations while riding on an airport shuttle bus or sitting near the galley on the airplane. Whenever I fly Alaska Airlines, the vast majority of flight attendants I encounter seem genuinely happy with their jobs, their coworkers, and their lives in general. This genuine happiness easily carries over to moments when they're serving passengers. On the other hand, I've often observed flight attendants from other airlines complaining about their jobs, coworkers, or personal lives. This attitude clearly impacts their quality of service. This may be one more reason why, in 2018, Alaska won the J.D. Power Award for highest customer satisfaction among traditional airlines in North America for the 11th year in a row.[119]

The effort required to bridge the gap between the display rules and actual emotions is known as "emotional labor." A little bit of emotional labor can be expected in any customer service role, but employees experiencing a large gap between their actual and displayed emotions over a prolonged period of time are highly susceptible to burnout. In much the same way that physical labor can tax our energy, exerting high amounts of emotional labor can leave people feeling physically and mentally exhausted.[120] Employees experiencing burnout ultimately leave their jobs, or—worse—continue in their positions long after they've stopped trying.

In 2016, I conducted a study on burnout risk among contact center employees in the United States. My research revealed that 74 percent of contact center agents were at risk of burnout! Unsurprisingly, the number one risk factor was when employees felt their company was not customer-focused.[121]

The costs of employee burnout and turnover are significant. Direct costs are fairly easy to calculate, such the as the cost of recruiting, hiring, and training new employees to replace the ones who leave. Indirect costs, such as lost productivity and decreased revenue due to poor performance, are much harder to calculate precisely but are often far greater than the direct costs.

I once worked with a hospital to help reduce turnover among its staff of 200 nurses. The annual turnover rate was 30 percent, meaning the hospital had to hire an average of 60 nurses every year to replace those who left. The direct cost of hiring and training replacements was $300,000 per year. However, the hospital's chief financial officer estimated the indirect costs associated with turnover—including lost productivity, lower patient satisfaction, and decreased levels of patient care—were as high as $3,000,000 per year, or 10 times as much as the direct costs. These indirect costs were hard to capture and measure, so an exact tally was elusive, but there was clearly a huge impact.

My work with this client focused on helping the hospital create a more positive and engaging environment. Management adjusted their hiring practices to find nurses who would be more likely to enjoy working there. They improved their training programs to provide nurses with skills to effectively handle stressful situations. The hospital's managers learned how to provide more positive feedback and recognition to improve the work climate. Within 18 months, these efforts paid off and their turnover rate had been cut in half.

Emotional labor was another obstacle I faced when I hung up on that customer many years ago. My dislike for my job and my bosses was so strong that it was getting harder and harder to go to work each day. I started getting sick more often and found myself becoming increasingly irritable around my employees, my friends, and even my wife. As a customer service manager, I was expected to model all of the display rules you'd expect from a service employee, but my true emotions rarely matched those expectations.

Eventually, I felt burned out and began to look for a new job with a better work environment. As luck would have it, I quickly received two job offers. One was as a Customer Service Manager for another call center; the other was as a Customer Service Trainer for a parking management company. The call center job paid 20 percent more and was in an industry I was familiar with, but a quick tour of the work environment told me their culture wouldn't be much different from the one I was trying to escape.

Despite the substantially lower salary, the customer service training position felt like my dream job. The person who would be my boss seemed wonderfully supportive and committed to creating an engaging work environment. In our interview, she spoke about her passion for the company and how they were truly committed to world class customer service. The potential coworkers I met during the interview process were all intelligent, dedicated people who seemed like they'd be fun to work with.

Choosing the training job over the call center management role was one of the easiest career decisions I've ever made. I distinctly remember making the call to accept my new job while on jury duty. The emotional labor of my soon-to-be-former job was so taxing that jury duty was a pleasant respite. Who'd imagine that being out of the office for three days while serving on a jury would feel like a vacation?

There are two strategies that companies can use to help their employees avoid the painful effects of high levels of emotional labor. The first is to create a positive and supportive work climate, which has already been discussed in this chapter. The second strategy is to help employees in high stress situations find ways to recover, much the same way you need to physically recover after a strenuous workout.

My favorite recovery technique is an "attitude anchor." An attitude anchor is something that secures your attitude in a positive place. For example, if I need help recovering from a stressful encounter with a customer, I might spend a few moments chatting with a trusted friend to lighten my mood and reset my attitude to a more positive frame of mind. Attitude anchors can also be used to maintain a healthy and positive outlook, such as regularly catching up with close friends regardless of whether I need their support in that moment.

Attitude anchors are inherently personal, so what works for one person may not work for someone else. Supervisors can help employees identify their own attitude anchors by having them make a list of "recovery" and "maintenance" anchors. I've listed a few of mine in Figure 10.1 as an example:

FIGURE 10.1: ATTITUDE ANCHORS

Recovery Anchors	Maintenance Anchors
• Talk to a trusted friend or coworker.	• Get regular exercise.
• Take a short walk and get some fresh air.	• Enjoy my morning coffee.
• Find a good joke or a cartoon.	• Listen to music.
• Take a deep breath and clear my mind.	• Relax while reading.
• Refocus on something positive.	• Spend time with friends and family.

Solution Summary:
Helping Employees Overcome Emotional Roadblocks

Customer service is an emotional job. There are highs associated with knowing you helped someone, and there are lows that come from working with challenging customers, coworkers, or bosses. Helping employees avoid or manage negative emotions is essential to creating an organization that consistently serves its customers at the highest level.

Here's a summary of the solutions offered in this chapter:

- Make employees, not customers, the top priority for the organization. This fosters a supportive work environment, promotes a sense of belonging, and encourages self-esteem.

- Meet with employees—in a supportive and non-judgmental way—after they've encountered an angry customer to help them learn from their experience and develop skills for handling similar situations in the future.
- Encourage employees to develop friendships with their coworkers so they'll find more enjoyment in their work environment.
- Ensure that supervisors apply a positive and supportive leadership style that encourages dedication and commitment from employees.
- Make your company a place where employees can easily leave their personal troubles behind and look forward to coming to work each day.
- Help employees identify their personal attitude anchors to help them maintain a positive outlook or recover from a negative encounter.

CHAPTER 10 NOTES

109 Kendra Cherry, with Steven Gans, MD. "How the Fight or Flight Response Works." *verywellmind*. July 11, 2018.

110 A. H. Maslow. "A Theory of Human Motivation." *Psychological Review*, Vol. 50, pgs 370–396. 1943.

111 Michael Sliter, Katherine Sliter, and Steve Jex. "The employee as a punching bag: The effect of multiple sources of incivility on employee withdrawal behavior and sales performance." *Journal of Organizational Behavior*, Vol. 33, Issue 1, pgs 121–139. John Wiley & Sons, Ltd. August 2011.

112 Interview with Herb Kelleher. "I Am American Business" series. Transcript on cnbc.com. Accessed October 11, 2018.

113 Elaine Hatfield and Richard L. Rapson. "Emotional contagion." *Current Directions in Pscychological Sciences*. Vol. 2, No. 3, pgs 96–99. June 1993.

114 Ulf Dimberg, Monika Thunberg, and Kurt Elmehed. "Unconscious Facial Reactions to Emotional Expressions." *Psychological Science*. Vol. 11, No. 1, pgs 86–89. January 2000.

115 "The Effect of Work Relationships on Organizational Culture and Commitment." *The Fall 2014 Workforce Mood Tracker*. Globoforce research report. 2014.

116   Zeynep Ton. *The Good Jobs Strategy: How the Smartest Companies Invest in Employees to Lower Costs and Boost Profits.* New Harvest. January 14, 2014.

117   Alicia A. Grandey. "Emotion Regulation in the Workplace: A New Way to Conceptualize Emotional Labor." *Journal of Occupational Health Psychology.* Vol. 5, No. 1, pgs 95–110. 2000.

118   You can view a number of PSA's ad campaigns on the online PSA history museum: www. jetpsa.com. One of the commercials is also easy to watch on YouTube: http://www.youtube.com/ watch?v=OOtv1lQ3Sgw. Accessed October 12, 2018.

119   "North America Airline Customer Satisfaction Improves for 7th Consecutive Year, J.D. Power Finds." J.D. Power press release. May 30, 2018.

120   Alicia A. Grandey. "Emotion Regulation in the Workplace: A New Way to Conceptualize Emotional Labor." *Journal of Occupational Health Psychology.* Vol. 5, No. 1, pgs 95–110. 2000.

121 Jeff Toister. "How to Battle Contact Center Agent Burnout." www.toistersolutions.com/ burnout. 2016.

CHAPTER 11

Casualties of Cost Consciousness

● ● ●

Seeing Customer Service as a Profit Generator Rather than a Cost Center

A number of years ago, I switched my home phone and internet service to the local cable company, because it promised faster web browsing and a lower price. The cable company's installer came to my house and got everything up and running in two hours.

However, a few days later, I noticed that my house alarm wasn't working properly. Apparently, the cable company installer hadn't reconnected the alarm to the new phone system, so my alarm couldn't connect to the alarm monitoring company. A second technician had to come spend another two hours finishing the installation.

Everything worked well for the next six months until a power outage knocked out my phone service. Even after power was restored, I still couldn't get a dial tone, so I called the cable company's technical support hotline and spent 30 minutes on the phone working through the various remedies suggested by the support representative. None of these attempts worked, so we scheduled a service call for a technician to come to my house.

The technician arrived within the promised four-hour window and went to work diagnosing the problem. He spent an hour and a half checking the phone system and even made several calls to his supervisor and other technicians to ask for help. The technician finally concluded that my loss of phone service was caused by a problem with my house alarm. He told me I'd need to call the alarm company to have them come out and fix it.

It took another series of phone calls and waiting through another four-hour service window for an alarm company technician to arrive. He spent two hours trying to find the problem until he decided the phone system was the culprit. The technician told me there was nothing he could do and the cable company needed to fix it. I'd now been without home phone service for several days, and I was starting to wonder if it would ever be restored. (Perhaps this is why far fewer people have a home phone today!)

After another aggravating runaround with the cable company's technical support hotline and scheduling myself to be home for yet another four-hour window, a third cable technician arrived at my house. I could immediately tell this guy was different from the previous technicians. He was a contractor rather than a cable company employee, and he seemed to have a lot more knowledge. It took him only a few minutes to figure out that my phone system had been configured incorrectly when it was originally installed, making it susceptible to failures like the one I was experiencing. He had everything corrected and my phone service restored inside of 30 minutes.

Counting the initial installation, it took four phone calls and four service appointments to install my home phone service.

The cable company's executives had tried to save money by creating a service strategy that assigned less experienced technicians to do the installation and initial repair. These technicians were paid less than their more skilled counterparts, so the projected savings was likely significant, but the strategy backfired and cost them substantially more than it should have. The company would have saved more money and avoided a huge customer service issue if it had sent out a capable technician to install the system right the first time.

In this chapter, we'll see that executives, just like their employees, face obstacles to delivering outstanding service. We'll explore how customer service leaders often use incomplete data when deciding how to deliver the most cost-effective service. We'll also examine common blunders executives make that lead to higher costs and lower revenue over the long term.

Fuzzy Math

My experience with the cable company isn't unusual. As of 2018, the cable industry as a whole was the lowest rated industry in terms of customer service on the American Customer Satisfaction Index.[122]

Part of the reason customers receive such poor service is that many cable companies focus on cost control when designing their service delivery systems. To them, the cost of providing customer service and technical support is a necessary evil, not an opportunity to create a long-term relationship with their customers.

Many of today's large cable companies have grown through acquisitions. When this happens, the two companies are typically using different billing systems and different technology to deliver cable, internet, and phone service to customers. Executives put off the decision to consolidate these disparate systems as long as possible because it can be very expensive, but operating multiple systems comes with its own set of challenges. For example, a customer moving from one side of town to the other might keep their account with the same cable company, but the move could trigger an avalanche of billing errors because the customer's new service area is managed with a completely different billing system than the old service area.

In my case, I was victimized by a tiered support structure that assigns the least-expensive person possible to try to fix a problem before escalating the issue to a more skilled, and therefore more costly, technician.

In theory, this tiered approach saves money, but that idea is based on incomplete financial data.

Using Salary.com for reasonable estimates for each position, an installation technician might make $28 per hour. Assuming each installation takes roughly two hours like mine did, the projected labor cost would be $56, plus $3.75 for a phone call with an inbound sales representative to establish service, for a total cost of $59.75.[123] (For the sake of simplicity, this estimate doesn't include equipment, overhead, trip time, vehicle costs, and many other expenses that would increase the final number.)

What executives don't always understand is how much they actually pay to make a complete installation when it's not done right the first time. Here's an estimate of the cost to install my phone system, again using Salary.com for reasonable estimates of average salaries for each position.[124]

$3.75	Inbound sales representative. 15 minutes @ $15 per hour
$15.00	Technical support representative. 50 minutes @ $18 per hour
$154.00	Installation & Repair technicians. 5.5 hours @ $28 per hour
$17.50	Senior Installation & Repair technician. 30 minutes @ $35 per hour
$75.00	Billing credit issued for phone service outage.
$265.25	**Total estimated cost**

What would have happened if the cable company had simply sent a qualified installer to do the job right the first time? Let's assume the senior level installer would still need two hours to conduct the initial installation. At a rate of $35 per hour, plus the $3.75 paid to the inbound sales rep, the total cost of doing the installation right the first time would be $73.75. In other words, by cutting corners and assigning less expensive but unqualified employees to do the job, the cable company inflated the total installation cost by $205.50—or 344 percent.

Executives often find it hard to quantify the cost of poor service experiences like mine, because the numbers are hidden in the financial reports they use to run their businesses. They can easily see how much revenue their company produced and how much their service technicians cost, but understanding the true cost of service is more elusive. At the time, the cable company managed its inbound sales, technical support, and installation departments via separate budgets, so executives did not have a clear line of sight on the total cost of an installation. It takes careful analysis to understand whether customer service processes are helping or hurting a company's profitability.

The chief financial officer of a now-defunct retailer once told me he couldn't see the importance of fixing a glitch that mispriced items on the company's website, leading to inaccurate inventory counts. To him, the expense of investing in new technology far outweighed the cost of a few errors. What he didn't understand was how those errors led to lost revenue, increased customer service costs, and ultimately caused customers to flee to competitors. In the end, his company was doomed because he and his fellow executives didn't have a deeper understanding of their profit and loss statement and didn't see the financial value in identifying and fixing systemic customer service failures.

Some companies try to manage customer service by tracking various metrics, but these efforts will fail if the metrics aren't correlated to customer satisfaction. For instance, many contact centers measure talk time—the average amount of time it takes to complete each phone call. The theory is that shorter phone calls are more economical since an employee can handle more per hour. More calls per hour means the company can hire fewer employees, lowering the effective cost per call.

Talk time is automatically tracked in most call centers, and supervisors can easily access this information and take action on it. An employee whose talk time is deemed too high can expect to hear from his or her supervisor and may even face disciplinary action. The inevitable result of emphasizing talk time is that employees focus on meeting a standard designed to control costs rather than solving customers' problems. This tends to increase call volume rather than reducing it. *Total* time on the phone, not the average time per call, is what really drives the cost of running a contact center.

According to the contact center research firm SQM Group, the average call center solves just 72 percent of their customers' problems on the first call. That means that 28 percent of calls handled by the typical call center are wasteful since a customer has to call at least once more to resolve their issue.[125]

I've talked to a number of contact center leaders who have shifted their agents' focus to first contact resolution rather than talk time. This has invariably resulted in improved first contact resolution, which in turn reduces call volume. The counterintuitive side effect is talk time remains the same and in some cases even declines!

Customer satisfaction is another blind spot for many executives. A 2015 study published by the International Customer Management Institute found that only 60 percent of contact centers capture customer satisfaction data and use it to improve service.[126] Without insight into what makes customers unhappy, companies risk wasting money by repeatedly subjecting customers to the same problems. They may even lose business when frustrated customers flee to a competitor.

There are many reasons why executives don't insist on capturing and analyzing customer feedback. One CEO I know doesn't like the consumer ratings site Yelp because he believes people only write reviews to air grievances. Another CEO told me he didn't feel a need to measure customer satisfaction because a few of his friends were saying good things, so he didn't think there were any problems. A third CEO told me he wanted to track customer service, but a closer examination revealed he was only interested in converting more inquiries into sales and didn't truly believe that customer satisfaction had an impact on his business.

Companies that want to use outstanding service to drive profits must have a commitment from top executives. Because executive leaders rely on data to make decisions, this must include a commitment to capture and analyze customer satisfaction data. This data could take many forms, including customer satisfaction surveys, tracking repeat businesses, or monitoring what customers are saying about your company via social media and online ratings sites.

One manufacturer used customer feedback to discover it was losing more than $1 million per year in preventable returns. These were products that worked perfectly well, but customers returned them because they couldn't figure out how to use them. Improving the product manual, adding resources to the company's website, and giving the support team better troubleshooting skills could drastically decrease the amount of returns.

The insurance company USAA is continuously one of the highest rated companies for customer service, and ranked number one in the Temkin Trust Ratings in 2018.[127] One of the keys to USAA's success is how the company combines customer feedback with other data sources to better understand customer needs and eliminate problems that stand in the way of serving customers profitably.

Julio Estevez-Breton, USAA's Vice President of Member and Market Insights, described USAA's approach this way: "Our relentless focus on doing right for our members drives good business outcomes. If you do the right things for your members, your employees will feel empowered. And if your employees are empowered and your customers are satisfied, that leads to good financial results."[128]

Less Is Often Less

It can be tempting for a business to try to increase profitability by reducing expenses. But businesses that focus on cutting costs without regard to customer satisfaction may inadvertently trigger a decline in revenue far beyond the benefits achieved by any cost savings.

I noticed an interesting sign one day while waiting for my sandwich at a convenience store deli. The large, handwritten sign was hanging above the self-serve coffee station:

NO FREE REFILLS!
(for any coffee)
NO EXCEPTIONS
(charged regular price for refills)

This unfriendly message was an attempt to control costs on two fronts. First, the store had installed a self-serve coffee station so the busy cashier didn't have to take extra time to pour coffee for customers. Second, the store didn't want to give away coffee, which would take up the cashier's time to refill the coffee dispensers more often and would ultimately increase the store's costs.

The sign may have saved a few dollars on the store's annual coffee bill, but it also drove customers away. The sign told customers, "We're too busy to help you, and we don't think you deserve any extra coffee." Perhaps the store manager didn't realize customers could get a free cup of coffee at the local hardware store, the bank, the auto shop, or any number of other places that understood how the goodwill generated by offering free coffee far outweighs the small expense. Here at the convenience store, customers have already bought the first cup, so why begrudge them a free refill?

Many retail department stores have cut back on labor expenses by reducing the number of associates on the sales floor. This move has undoubtedly yielded some savings, but the downside is that there are fewer employees helping customers make a selection, find the right size, or add additional items to the sale. In some cases, customers even have to hunt for a cashier just to ring up a purchase. Many of those customers simply give up and do their shopping online or at another store.

Restaurants suffer from the same challenge. Each fall, my Saturdays are typically spent at college football watch parties organized by local alumni clubs and held at various sports bars. A good server can keep a crowd happy—and add to their restaurant's bottom line—over the course of the four-hour game by periodically checking in to refill sodas and offering to take another food or drink order. However, when restaurants cut back on staff, it's harder for servers to provide prompt, personal attention for all their tables at these football watch parties. There have been many times when people in our group have decided against ordering an extra plate of nachos or one more beer because it took too long for our busy server to check on us.

Some companies have tried to reduce their reliance on costly employees by investing in self-service technology, but this strategy backfires if the technology isn't easy to use or becomes a source of customer frustration. Virtually all contact centers rely on an automated phone menu as a way of routing customer calls and providing self-service options. This technology saves companies a few dollars by reducing the number of call center representatives needed, but it's also a near-universal source of customer aggravation.

Customers are frustrated with the endless arrays of options and automated voice-driven menus that never seem to work properly. When they finally do get someone on the phone, they're often asked to provide the same account number they were just required to punch in on the phone system. There are even websites, such as GetHuman (www.gethuman.com), that offer tips and shortcuts for getting a live person on the phone.

Self-service kiosks have become increasingly prevalent in places such as grocery stores, airports, and parking facilities. In some instances, the speed and convenience offered by these self-service options have been a real benefit to customers. In other instances, they can be costly. One study found that 20 percent of customers admitted to stealing items when using grocery store self-checkout stations, and reported that stores lose an average of $.85 in theft per transaction.[129]

Organizations committed to outstanding service avoid cutting costs for the sake of reducing expenses alone. They understand the impact of cost-cutting measures on customer service, including the implications for lost revenue and efficiency. In some cases, the return on investment is so hard to calculate that leaders simply have to trust that doing the right thing for their customers will pay off in the long run.

I once delivered a customer service training class in a movie theater at a shopping mall. The participants were employees of the mall's parking garage, and the theater manager let us use the room at no cost. The manager even provided free popcorn and soft drinks for everyone to enjoy. The class, which included a training video shown on the big screen, was a memorable experience for everyone.

At first glance, it might not seem like the theater manager had much to gain by waiving the theater rental fee, giving us free concessions, and paying employees to come in early to serve us. Sure, a better parking experience for theater-goers might generate a little extra revenue, but we were going to train our employees anyway. Yet this move paid off in the fantastic experience enjoyed by the 50 employees who attended the class. Those 50 employees were potential customers, along with their friends and family members who heard about the wonderful time they had at the customer service training hosted by the theater.

Some investments do have a clear impact. When I shop at Bath and Body Works to buy a gift for my wife, I always feel out of my element until I'm approached by a helpful sales associate. The company's cheerful salespeople help me make selections that always end up pleasing my wife, and their expert suggestive selling skills frequently entice me to purchase more than I'd originally intended to buy. Bath and Body Works views its associates as people who generate revenue and promote repeat business, not as expenses to be minimized.

Self-service technology can also pay off if companies understand that the human element is still extremely important. I'm a fan of Mimeo. com, an on-demand printing company that lets you upload documents to its website, select the binding and finishing options you want, and then delivers a fantastically high-quality finished product as early as the next morning. The website is easy to use, and there's always a customer service rep available if I need assistance.

Things have gone perfectly every time I've used Mimeo.com with just two exceptions. On one occasion, I uploaded a file in a format that didn't print very well, and the document was unusable. Thankfully, a helpful customer service rep walked me through the process of creating a better file and didn't charge me for the replacement order, even though it was my own error.

The second time something went wrong was when the delivery driver for a third-party shipping company accidentally delivered my order to the wrong address. It took some detective work to find out what happened since the delivery company's records indicated the order had been delivered correctly, but a Mimeo customer service rep eventually sent out a replacement order at no charge. In both instances, it was human (and not Mimeo's) error that caused the problem. It was also a human who quickly solved each problem I experienced, which is why I remain a loyal Mimeo customer.

Problems can and will happen, but anything short of a swift resolution will infuriate customers and cause them to take their business elsewhere. In many cases, this means a friendly, well-trained person must be available to quickly assist a customer in need. A 2017 study commissioned by Microsoft found that 81 percent of U.S. customers preferred the telephone when contacting a company for assistance.[130] It might be cheaper for Mimeo to provide layers of phone menus and self-serve options to encourage me to resolve my problem without assistance from an expensive employee, but spending a little more on customer service allows Mimeo to earn my continued business even when I do encounter an occasional challenge.

Short-Term Gains that Spread Customer Ill Will

A number of years ago, I had to get the water pump replaced on my trusty Honda Accord. When I picked up the car from the repair shop, I noticed the final bill was several hundred dollars higher than the estimate. A closer look revealed that the mechanic had replaced my timing belt, even though I didn't request it and it hadn't been included in the estimate.

I asked to speak to the manager and showed him both my estimate and the repair bill. His initial response was to nonchalantly explain that they always replaced the timing belt when they replaced a water pump. He didn't know why this wasn't included in the original estimate or why nobody from the shop had gotten my permission before adding such an expensive item, but he didn't seem to understand why this was a problem. Instead, he just shrugged and insisted that was their normal procedure.

Replacing a timing belt is an expensive repair, and I had just gotten this done a few months earlier. If there was a problem with the belt, the replacement should have been covered under warranty. If there wasn't anything wrong with the belt, then the manager was hoping I wouldn't put up too much of a fight when he tried to gouge me for a few hundred dollars.

I calmly asked the manager if there had been anything wrong with the timing belt the mechanic had replaced. He couldn't answer that question, so I gave him two options. He could either reinstall my old timing belt or give me the new one for free. He reluctantly decided to take the timing belt replacement off the bill.

This unethical attempt to pad their revenue cost the repair shop more than the price of the part and the mechanic's labor. My wife and I had both been taking our cars to this shop, but after this incident, we vowed never to return. I imagine this type of business practice eventually caught up to them, because they are no longer in business.

The pursuit of revenue without regard to customer satisfaction led the video streaming and DVD rental company Netflix to make not just one, but two colossal service blunders in 2011. It started when the company announced a 60 percent price increase on July 12 in an email sent to subscribers and a post on the company blog. The backlash from surprised and outraged customers generated a wave of negative press for the company and prompted many to cancel their service.[131]

Customers were still fuming about the price hike when Netflix made its second blunder. On September 18, Netflix CEO Reed Hastings announced on the Netflix blog that the company was separating its online video streaming and DVD rental services into two separate businesses. This move would require customers to maintain one account to manage and pay for their online streaming and a separate account to manage and pay for their DVD rentals. Hastings explained the move was necessary because the two services had different cost structures and marketing challenges. He also offered an apology for the way Netflix communicated the price increase it announced earlier in the year, but defended the move as a necessary business decision.[132]

This time, consumer outrage was so deafening that Netflix reversed its plans to separate video streaming and DVD rentals into separate businesses. However, the damage had already been done. Netflix lost 800,000 subscribers and its stock declined 75 percent in the third quarter of 2011. The company also suffered a 14 percent decrease in customer satisfaction on the 2011 American Customer Satisfaction Index, one of the most dramatic one-year declines ever recorded.[133]

I was one of the Netflix subscribers affected by the 60 percent price increase. Like many customers, I considered canceling my service and tried to find a reasonable alternative. My surprising conclusion was that even after the price increase, Netflix still offered the best deal for the services I used.

The rate hike might have been the product of sound financial and marketplace analysis, but it alienated customers unnecessarily when Hastings and his executive team didn't consider the strong emotional reaction such a large price increase would generate. As a result of my analysis, I remained a Netflix member, but I stopped referring them or giving gift subscriptions as I had in the past.

Some companies have resorted to new fees as a way of raising revenue without increasing advertised prices. Airlines have been steadily implementing fees for many things that used to be free, such as checked bags, seat assignments, and in-flight snacks. Event ticketing companies charge convenience fees, transaction fees, and ticket delivery fees on top of the ticket prices. Hotels assess internet fees, resort fees, and charge for bottled water in addition to the room rate. The list goes on and on.

These fees can provide much-needed revenue, especially in industries that consistently struggle to be profitable—such as airlines. However, they can also alienate customers and cost companies business. For instance, in July 2018, American Airlines changed its policy to allow passengers traveling on "basic economy" fares to bring aboard a free carry-on bag rather than paying $25 under American's previous policy. The airline's CEO, Doug Parker, told investors, "There are now filters on things like Google search that ask you if you want to bring a carry-on, and if you say yes, the American flights don't show up nearly as high as they did before."[134]

While executives face pressure from shareholders to find innovative ways to grow revenue, smart companies recognize that outstanding customer service can lead to better results in the long run. Customer service leaders should evaluate any plan to raise prices or implement new fees against the potential impact on customer retention, revenue per customer, and referrals. Failure to consider the full impact can result in customer defections and lost sales.

For example, I've used a customer relationship management software program called Highrise HQ for many years. A subscription for my particular plan was $29 per month when I first signed up. Today, that same plan is $49 per month, but I still pay $29. Highrise promotes customer loyalty by holding prices steady for existing customers.

I also pay a monthly subscription fee for online accounting software. This company raises its prices at least once per year, and every time it does, I'm prompted to search for alternatives. The few customer service interactions I've had with the company over the years have been decent, but not spectacular enough for me to remain unquestionably loyal no matter how much the product costs.

When customer-focused companies do increase prices or add new fees, they often find a way to add additional value for customers. In 2018, internet retailer Amazon raised the cost of its Prime service to $119 per year. Prime members receive free shipping, access to Amazon's video streaming service, and many more benefits that more than pay for the annual cost for most customers.[135] Amazon frequently adds new member benefits, such as a 10 percent discount for Prime members at Amazon's grocery chain, Whole Foods, which was announced in June 2018.[136] Amazon also uses revenue from Prime subscriptions to keep its prices as low as possible, with at least one analysis suggesting the company actually makes the bulk of its profits from Prime subscriptions while *losing* money on the products it sells because its prices are so low.[137]

The volume discount chain Costco is another business that profitably combines outstanding service with exceptionally low prices by charging customers a membership fee. Like Amazon, Costco makes its profits on memberships, so it's able to keep prices as low as possible.[138]

There's a good chance you've heard quite a few friends talking about the ease of doing business with Amazon or a great deal they got at Costco. Referrals like that are free advertising for businesses. Companies that provide great value by keeping prices reasonable and delivering outstanding service are much more likely to have customers refer new customers. On the other hand, negative publicity like Netflix experienced in reaction to their price increase can drive potential customers away. (In fairness to Netflix and Reed Hastings, the company apparently learned from its experience and has since restored its reputation as an affordable source of convenient entertainment.)

Executives can be tempted to offer discounts to lure in new customers, but low prices alone won't keep your customers happy. What customers really want is value. This means a good product backed by good service at a fair price.

Look carefully and you can probably find a better price for many of the products sold on Amazon. But Amazon wins by making it incredibly convenient for you to find what you want, place an order, and in some cases, get it delivered that same day. And if something goes wrong or you don't like what you purchased, returning it for a refund or exchange is almost as easy as placing the order.

In 2004, I was elected to serve a two-year term as Membership Director for the San Diego chapter of the American Society for Training and Development, a professional association for corporate trainers (it's now known as the Association for Talent Development). During my two-year term, we increased chapter membership by 67 percent without any advertising, discounts, or special promotions. Instead, our leadership team relied on referrals to help the organization grow. We worked diligently to engage members on a personal level, discover their interests, and provide valuable services in return for their membership dues so they would encourage their colleagues to join the chapter, too.

Solution Summary:
How to Position Customer Service as a Profit Generator

It can be difficult for executives to consider the impact on customer service when making strategic decisions about their companies. They often lack direct contact with customers, and the limited customer service data they have is not as comprehensive, easy to understand, or reliable as the financial reports they're so comfortable using. However, leaders must understand that outstanding customer service isn't a cost to be minimized; it's an investment in future profitability.

Here's a summary of the solutions discussed in this chapter:

- Executives must capture and analyze customer satisfaction data to ensure strategic decisions aren't based solely on financial metrics.
- Customer service leaders should dig deeper into their financial statements to understand the true cost of poor customer service.
- The long-term benefit of customer service investments should be

fully understood before implementing cost-cutting measures that might drive customers away.

- Investing in the right number of qualified, well-trained employees pays off when those employees are able to drive sales and customer satisfaction.
- Self-service technology can be tempting due to promised cost savings, but the expense of lost customers and lost revenue can be high if the technology doesn't function properly or customers find it irritating or difficult to use.
- Executives should carefully consider the impact of any price or fee increase on customer retention, revenue per customer, and referrals before making a final decision.

CHAPTER 11 NOTES

122 The American Customer Satisfaction Index. http://theacsi.org/national-economic-indicator/national-sector-and-industry-results. Accessed August 11, 2018.

123 Salary data from www.salary.com. Accessed October 18, 2018.

124 Salary data from www.salary.com. Accessed October 18, 2018.

125 "Top 5 Reasons to Improve First Contact Resolution." SQM Group. August 24, 2017.

126 "Collapse of the Cost Center: Driving Contact Center Profitability." International Customer Management Institute. 2015.

127 2018 Temkin Trust ratings. https://temkingroup.com/temkin-ratings/temkin-trust-ratings. Accessed August 11, 2018.

128 "When Customers Love Their Bank, with USAA's Julio Estevez-Breton." *Net Promoter System Podcast.* July 26, 2018.

129 Rene Chun. "The Banana Trick and Other Acts of Self-Checkout Thievery." *The Atlantic.* March 2018.

130 "Global State of Multichannel Customer Service Report." Microsoft research report. 2017.

131 Jessica Becker. "Netflix Introduces New Plans and Announces Price Changes." *Netflix US & Canada blog.* July 12, 2011.

132 Reed Hastings. "An Explanation and Some Reflections." *Netflix US & Canada blog.* September 18, 2011.

133   Claes Fornell. "ACSI Commentary February 2012." *The American Customer Satisfaction Index.* February 21, 2012.

134   Dawn Gilbertson. "American Airlines now allows free carry-on bag for 'basic economy' passengers." *USA Today.* July 26, 2018.

135   Joseph Pisani. "Amazon raising price of annual Prime membership to $119." *AP News.* April 26, 2018.

136   Andy Beatman. "New benefit for Prime Members at Whole Foods Market." Amazon.com. June 26, 2018.

137   Thomas H. Kee Jr. "Amazon Is Losing Billions From Its Retail Business and Rivals Should Be Scared." *The Street.* April 27, 2018.

138   Daniel B. Kline. "How Costco Wholesale Corporation Makes Most of Its Money." *The Motley Fool.* May 5, 2017.

PART III

Putting Lessons Into Action

CHAPTER 12

Getting Started

● ● ●

One of my favorite training exercises to use with customer service leaders is called the "Road Trip Activity." I tell the group they have one minute to brainstorm items they'd take with them on a road trip, and I encourage them to work with the people sitting near them. "Is everyone ready?" I ask before starting the timer. They're always eager to get started.

The participants aren't given any rules other than my request to brainstorm, yet their behavior is remarkably consistent every time I run this activity. People quickly form small groups and excitedly share ideas. Most people begin with the assumption that the activity is a competition and the team that brainstorms the most items will win. One person in each group inevitably takes charge of writing down their ideas.

About 30 seconds into the exercise, it dawns on one or two people that nobody asked a very important question. Gradually a few others realize it too. However, most people complete the activity without noticing they're missing the most important piece of information.

Where are we going?

After the minute is up, I ask everyone to share how many items they came up with. Even then, there are still some groups that haven't caught on as they excitedly share their totals and look around the room to see if they brainstormed the most items. Finally, someone in the class asks the most important question out loud: "Where are we going?" You can almost see the light bulbs go on over everyone's head.

I run the activity a second time, but now I give them a specific destination—such as a theme park, a baseball game, or the beach—a few hours' drive from where the class is being held. Several items on the second list carry over from the first, but there are also new items essential to enjoying the destination, such as bringing a bathing suit and a towel to a day at the beach. The second list is almost always much shorter than the first.

This activity demonstrates how easy it is to engage in action without having a clear objective. When we're extremely busy, it feels like we're getting something done, even when we're heading in the wrong direction or just spinning around in circles. We can only avoid this trap when we know where we're headed before we start our journey. Only then can we make the preparations that will ensure we get where we want to be.

In this final chapter, we'll focus on practical ways to implement the ideas and advice described in previous chapters. We'll start by exploring some of the pitfalls that can cause a customer service initiative to fail. Next, we'll look at three steps organizations can take to overcome the obstacles outlined in this book and achieve consistently positive results. Finally, I'll offer one last reminder that outstanding customer service employees may already be working for your company. All you need to do is help them be great!

What to Know Before You Get Started

It's important to know why customer service initiatives fail before you get started on the journey to improve service in your own organization. This will help you avoid those mistakes and chart a course toward success.

The first cause of failure is what I call "Harvard Business Review management." This is when a leader reads about the latest management trend in *Harvard Business Review* or another leading management publication and decides to implement the idea in their organization without fully understanding the concept or what's required to make it succeed. The inevitable result of this approach is the leader severely underestimating the commitment and resources necessary to obtain the same results described in the magazine article or business book.

As a national account manager for a company selling uniforms, it was my job to work with my clients to keep them happy and grow their business. One day, the general manager of our group announced his decision to reorganize all the account managers and support staff into self-directed teams. The general manager felt this approach would allow us to improve client service and increase sales by working in small teams focused on specific industries.

The unintended result of his decision was inefficiency, declining sales, and low morale—exactly the opposite of what he'd anticipated. People who were used to working independently, even to the point of competing with coworkers for territory and sales leads, were now expected to collaborate, but were given no training on how to do so. The reorganization also angered many customers who were upset at suddenly being assigned a new account manager. Within six months, the business unit's performance was so bad that the company began laying people off or transferring them to other departments. A year later, the entire group was gone.

The concept of self-directed work teams was a hot management trend when the general manager made his decision. It was the subject of countless magazine articles and case studies that profiled companies implementing this concept with great success. In the end, the initiative failed because the general manager announced the strategy but did little to ensure it was implemented successfully.

This general manager was not alone in his actions. Many executives pass around an interesting article to their teams with a note exclaiming, "Let's do this!" Some leaders distribute books to their managers as part of an ad-hoc leadership book club. (Is that how you came to read this book?)

The problem with this approach is that it's just the *beginning* of the journey rather than the end. Simply announcing "Teams!" doesn't mean everyone will suddenly begin working in well-coordinated groups to the immense delight of their customers. Proclaiming "Customers are our number one priority!" won't change a thing until things are actually changed.

Another way for a customer service initiative to fail is to make it a project that people work on temporarily or in their spare time. This arrangement implies that customer service is an afterthought rather than a real priority. It makes it easy for the initiative to be set aside when operational issues arise or the management team gets distracted by the next management fad.

Outstanding customer service needs to be hardwired into the way your company does business if you want your organization's service to consistently reach that level. It should be factored into strategic decisions, as we discussed in Chapter 11. It must be ingrained in the culture that was described in Chapter 3, and considered when developing policies and procedures, as we covered in Chapter 6. In my experience as a customer service consultant, this is the clear difference between companies whose initiatives succeed and those whose initiatives fail.

Yet one more way for a customer service initiative to fail is when it starts with training, since the training is implemented before critical decisions are made. In their book *Courageous Training*, employee performance experts Robert Brinkerhoff and Tom Mooney state that companies must first set clear goals, identify the actions employees need to take to achieve those goals, and only then determine what training is needed to help employees achieve the desired performance. Companies that launch training programs without setting goals or clearly defining desired employee behaviors don't really know what training needs to be offered or why it's important.[139]

I often respond to training requests from my clients by asking, "How will we know if this training program is successful?" The question sparks an important conversation when my clients haven't thought through how training connects to business results. This discussion usually results in a much smaller and more focused training plan. And much like the "Road Trip Activity," the plan often includes elements that wouldn't have been incorporated if we'd started training without verifying the objectives.

The First Three Steps in the Journey to Outstanding Service

Every journey begins with the first step. In this case, I'll offer you the first three—with the caveat that they're easy to understand in concept, but can be difficult to implement and master.

1. Clearly define outstanding service,
2. Use this definition as a compass to guide everything you do, and
3. Reinforce constantly.

STEP 1: CLEARLY DEFINE OUTSTANDING SERVICE.

What does outstanding service mean to your organization or your department?

This definition is the compass that guides your strategy, your decisions, and your culture. We covered the hallmarks of a good definition in Chapter 3, when we discussed the importance of creating a customer-focused culture, but the three characteristics bear repeating here.

1. The definition is simple and easily understood.
2. It describes the type of service we want to achieve for our customers.
3. It reflects both who we are now and who we aspire to be in the future.

Here are a few examples from some of the success stories described earlier in the book[140]:

- *Southwest Airlines*: The mission of Southwest Airlines is dedication to the highest quality of Customer Service delivered with a sense of warmth, friendliness, individual pride, and Company Spirit.
- *True Value*: Our vision: to help every True Value be the best hardware store in town.
- *L.L.Bean*: Sell good merchandise at a reasonable profit, treat your customers like human beings, and they will always come back for more.
- *REI*: Our core purpose is to inspire, educate, and outfit people for a lifetime of outdoor adventure and stewardship.
- *Starbucks*: Our mission: to inspire and nurture the human spirit— one person, one cup and one neighborhood at a time.

Outstanding service can be defined by a mission statement, a vision, a set of company values, a motto, a slogan, a credo, or anything else that's important to the organization and its employees. There's no one right way to do it. All that matters is that outstanding service is clearly defined and that the definition is infused into everything the company does.

STEP 2: USE THIS DEFINITION AS A COMPASS TO GUIDE EVERYTHING YOU DO.

Your definition of outstanding customer service should be considered whenever a decision has an impact on customer service. Chapters 2 through 11 each outline a specific obstacle that employees, teams, or organizations may face. Below are 10 questions to help you assess, chapter by chapter, whether you're heading in the right direction or if you need to adjust course. For each "No" answer, I recommend revisiting the corresponding chapter to identify the actions necessary to get back on track.

1. Do we make it easy for our customers to be right? (Chapter 2)
2. Do we have a strong, customer-focused culture? (Chapter 3)
3. Do our employees love to provide the level of service they're asked to give their customers? (Chapter 4)
4. Are employees able to serve their customers without feeling caught between what the company wants them to do and what the customer desires? (Chapter 5)
5. Do our policies, procedures, and workflows make it easy for our employees to delight our customers? (Chapter 6)
6. Are employees able to focus their attention on providing the highest level of customer service? (Chapter 7)
7. Do employees clearly understand that customer service is their top priority? (Chapter 8)
8. Are employees given the tools and guidance necessary to help them empathize with their customers? (Chapter 9)
9. Does our workplace actively encourage positive feelings and emotions? (Chapter 10)
10. Do our leaders use customer service metrics as a guide when making strategic decisions? (Chapter 11)

STEP 3: REINFORCE CONSTANTLY.

The third step in the journey is a never-ending process of constantly reinforcing customer service expectations with employees. Employees understand the importance of an activity or a cultural value by how it's emphasized.

I once knew a manager whose sole action to help employees improve their level of service was a tersely-worded memo attached to their paychecks. He never provided training, coaching, or reinforcement of any kind, so it should have been no surprise that performance never improved. Despite the manager's strongly-worded memo, his actions suggested that customer service really wasn't that important.

Leaders who make customer service a priority take every opportunity to reinforce the message with their employees. Here are just a few examples illustrating how this can be done.

- Hold regular meetings to discuss customer service with employees.
- Post visual customer service reminders such as illustrative posters.
- Frequently provide employees with individual feedback.
- Give employees regular updates on their progress toward customer service goals.
- Deliver periodic refresher courses to reinforce customer service skills.
- Organize committees to tackle specific customer service challenges.
- Pick a new customer service skill to focus on each week as a way to provide ongoing reminders and maintain constant awareness. (You can sign up for my free Customer Service Tip of the Week at www.toistersolutions.com/tips, and use it to help with this step.)

A Final Note: Your Worst Employee Might Be Your Best

I'll never forget my first assignment as a Training Supervisor at a catalog company. On my first day on the job, I was asked to investigate problems with one of my night shift trainers, whom we'll call Nicole (not her real name). I was given two weeks to report back to my boss with either a decision to fire Nicole or a plan to improve her performance.

It was clear my boss thought Nicole would need to be fired. She was concerned that Nicole was insubordinate and a divisive influence on the team. She'd heard complaints that Nicole refused to use some of the training materials all our trainers were required to use. Some of the other trainers had complained that Nicole wasn't a team player, and my boss had made similar observations herself.

My team was responsible for training the customer service

representatives who worked in two of the company's contact centers, which were about ten miles apart. Most of the department, including my boss, worked in the larger of the two facilities, but Nicole worked in the smaller contact center. The night shift ran from 4:00 pm to midnight, so she had infrequent contact with my boss and with the department's other trainers.

The natural starting point for my assignment was to spend some time with Nicole so I could make an assessment based on my own observations. Nicole was a single mother who worked the night shift in order to care for her daughter during the day and have her mother watch her daughter while she went to work at night. As a young supervisor, I was nervous about making a decision that would have such a big impact on someone's livelihood. At the same time, I wanted to be good at my job and please my boss, and I knew my boss expected me to be able to make tough decisions.

It didn't take much time with Nicole to identify the major obstacles that hindered her performance. One obstacle was the training material Nicole was expected to use. She didn't deny that there were some materials she refused to use in her training classes, but she explained that those materials were out of date and didn't reflect the contact center's current policies. Nicole had repeatedly asked for updated materials from the employee responsible for maintaining the training materials in all our contact centers, but the documentation specialist had informed Nicole she was three months behind on her work and couldn't make the requested changes any time soon.

This left Nicole with the choice to either use outdated materials in her classes, or make adjustments on her own so she could train new hires on current policies. She knew the contact center supervisors her trainees would report to after training expected their employees to be fully trained on current policies, so her credibility would be questioned if she used the old materials. Her decision to make her own materials came from a refusal to let the documentation specialist's backlog be an excuse for not properly training new employees. Interestingly, it was the documentation specialist who had been complaining to my boss about Nicole's refusal to use the old materials.

Another obstacle was Nicole's schedule. Our department held a team meeting at the larger contact center every Thursday, and all the trainers were expected to attend. The meeting started at 4:00 pm, when the second shift arrived, and typically lasted until 5:00 pm. Nicole's classes ran from 6:00 pm to midnight. It was a 30-minute drive between contact centers at that time of day, so that left her only half an hour to prepare for the evening's class. This understandably put her in a rush to leave the weekly meeting, but her coworkers mistook her haste as an unwillingness to create personal connections with the rest of the team.

After a short investigation, I went back to my boss and delivered a surprising report. Nicole shouldn't be fired. In fact, she was one of our best trainers!

Fixing the negative perceptions about Nicole's performance took some time, but the solutions were simple. The documentation specialist reported to my boss, so my boss directed her to reprioritize her work to make the necessary updates to the training materials. I allowed Nicole to attend the weekly meeting via conference call so she'd have enough time to prepare for that evening's class. I also adjusted Nicole's schedule so she occasionally had a few days when she wasn't training and could create stronger relationships with her colleagues by working with them on special projects.

This experience stayed with me because it started with the assumption that Nicole was a rogue employee with a bad attitude who needed to be fired. Yet it turned out that she was someone who cared deeply about doing a great job. She just needed help to remove the obstacles that stood in her way. Nicole flourished once the path to success was cleared. In fact, she was promoted into my boss's job just five years later!

There are countless employees like Nicole whose hidden potential is just waiting to be uncovered. It's hard to assess the capabilities of these employees when significant obstacles remain in place, and the challenges they face are sometimes so severe that poor service is the inevitable result. Of course there are a few people who aren't able to improve under any circumstances, but the vast majority of customer service employees can do great things when given the opportunity.

I believe the fundamental mission for every customer service leader is to help their employees serve customers at the highest level. This involves identifying and removing the obstacles that stand in their way. It takes patience and understanding, because even the best of us sometimes falter.

Above all else, customer service leaders must remember that while customer service can be difficult, their job is to make great performance easy.

CHAPTER 12 NOTES

139 Tom Mooney and Robert O. Brinkerhoff. *Courageous Training: Bold Actions for Business Results.* Berrett-Koehler Publishers, Inc., San Francisco, 2008.

140 All of these examples came from the respective companies' websites: www.southwest.com, www.truevaluecompany.com, www.llbean.com, www.rei.com, and www.starbucks.com.

● ● ●

Index

54195376R00126

Made in the USA
Columbia, SC
29 March 2019